"Too often, the pastor's family lives with wei[...] secrets. Dad has been called—summoned by [...] congregation—to undershepherd a flock of s[...] pastor's wife and children live under expectat[...] ily in the church. PKs are born into a burden and a blessing that they did not choose but in God's providence was chosen for them. And under the spotlight, they confront the world, the flesh, and the devil. This excellent and balanced volume gives biblical words, categories, and concepts to these real burdens. Every chapter in this book is worth its weight. And every chapter unearths an important truth—when God calls a man to the office of teaching elder (pastor), He intends a blessing for each member of his family. God never overlooks the obedience of children. While that blessing may have sharp edges and lonely days, under the light of the gospel and the love of God, it bears fruit for the child, the church, and the world.

—Rosaria Butterfield, wife of Kent Butterfield, pastor of the First Reformed Presbyterian Church of Durham, North Carolina; and homeschooling mother and grandmother

"Catherine Stewart, who edited the helpful book *Letters to Pastors' Wives*, has assembled another timely volume with an impressive list of contributors called *Surviving the Fishbowl: Letters to Pastors' Kids*. Every pastoral family will resonate with the topics covered and find wisdom and encouragement for facing the challenges that children encounter in the course of ministry life."

—Ligon Duncan, chancellor and CEO, Reformed Theological Seminary

"The latest collection from Catherine Stewart is another gem. How I wish I had this volume while our three PKs were growing up. Not to worry: now this resource should be on every gift list for every pastor's home. It is practical, biblical, and lively and features a faculty of wise and experienced parents. Having known many of the children discussed in this book and their parents, who write unique epistles to pastors' kids, I find that this fine and timely book oozes authenticity. If you love your pastor, share this book with his children!"

—David Hall, senior pastor, Midway Presbyterian Church (PCA), Powder Springs, Georgia

"I'm not sure I've seen a book quite like this one, and it's curious why that is so. Pastors' kids are certainly in a fishbowl, and these letters covering every imaginable issue are the perfect antidote for both parents and children. Cleverly conceived and disarmingly candid, this book is sure to do a great deal of good. I nominate it as book of the year!"

SURVIVING THE FISHBOWL

SURVIVING THE
FISHBOWL

LETTERS TO PASTORS' KIDS

Edited by
Catherine Stewart

Reformation Heritage Books
Grand Rapids, Michigan

Reformation Heritage Books
2965 Leonard St. NE
Grand Rapids, MI 49525
616–977–0889
orders@heritagebooks.org
www.heritagebooks.org

The views expressed in this book are entirely those of the individual writer and do not represent the opinions or convictions of the other contributors.

Printed in the United States of America
21 22 23 24 25 26/10 9 8 7 6 5 4 3 2 1

Library of Congress Cataloging-in-Publication Data

Names: Stewart, Catherine J., 1974- editor.
Title: Surviving the fishbowl : letters to pastors' kids / edited by Catherine Stewart.
Description: Grand Rapids, Michigan : Reformation Heritage Books, [2021]
Identifiers: LCCN 2020052546 (print) | LCCN 2020052547 (ebook) | ISBN 9781601788344 (paperback) | ISBN 9781601788351 (epub)
Subjects: LCSH: Children of clergy.
Classification: LCC BV4396 .S88 2021 (print) | LCC BV4396 (ebook) | DDC 248.8/2—dc23
LC record available at https://lccn.loc.gov/2020052546
LC ebook record available at https://lccn.loc.gov/2020052547

For additional Reformed literature, request a free book list from Reformation Heritage Books at the above regular or email address.

**Hannah, Benjamin, Eleah Marie, Josiah,
Samuel, and Eliza Kate,**

*For you we prayed. For you we labored. For you we give thanks.
Given the chance, you might not have chosen the life of a pastor's kid,
but when God chose it for you, He enriched our lives beyond measure.
May He dog your steps with mercy and kindness always. Press on!*

—Catherine Stewart, editor

CONTENTS

FOREWORD

Compelled by the testimony of Scripture, we must insist that a call to pastoral ministry rests only upon the man whom God has equipped and qualified for the work of the gospel. Yet we must also confess, in light of the unavoidable evidence of personal experience, that the implications of that call reach well beyond him, sweeping his wife and children along with it.

Their lives are so intimately intertwined with his that his ministry joys and sorrows, his pastoral trials and triumphs are, at least in some measure, theirs as well. With him they get to see, from a uniquely privileged vantage point, the many ways in which the Spirit of Christ is busy transforming human lives as the Word of God is proclaimed. Knowing Dad as they do, our children see the faded glory of a fallen man made in God's image, redeemed by Jesus Christ, and called to preach the gospel. They live in close proximity to his gifts and graces. With his besetting sins and fleshly liabilities, they are all too familiar. And so when the Lord uses us, all our liabilities notwithstanding, our children are being shown the grace of God deploying an often ignoble and weak thing (1 Cor. 1:26 and the verses following) in the accomplishment of His glorious design. There is an opportunity afforded to pastors' children to understand that, while "Dad" ought never to be set upon a pedestal, yet, despite his many failings, even he can be God's instrument for good. A pastor can be a living demonstration of the power of God to His children, encouraging them never to rule themselves beyond the reach of grace, nor to exclude themselves from the possibility of usefulness in

Christian service. I want my boys to conclude, as they enter into manhood, "If God used *my* dad, he can certainly use *me*."

So, the children of a minister have a privileged access to the life of a man whom God has called to the ministry of the Word and prayer. And yet, with this privilege come many temptations. Unreasonable expectations from congregants (or even from Mom and Dad) can drive a pastor's child to rebel or to become a practiced Pharisee. A carefully cultivated air of churchy moralism, tinctured with all the right vocabulary and a meekly compliant spirit, easily becomes a strategy to keep the judgments of others at bay. Disillusionment with the church, with whom a needy teenager must compete for her father's attention and time, can slowly slide into disillusionment with the gospel itself. Dad's hypocrisy cannot be hidden from his children when he says one thing in the pulpit but does another at home. His short temper under stress, his prayerlessness, his readiness to respond to the pastoral needs of the flock while missing the hurting hearts of his own household—these describe the minefield of a pastor's family life.

And with these temptations come many weighty responsibilities. Pastors' children see and hear much more than most church members ever will, and their ability to cope with the infidelities and fault lines that run through every church is too often assumed but rarely cultivated. Where the pastor is faithful at home, the duty of his children to believe the gospel and live for Christ is heightened beyond that of other children. Pastors' children have greater privileges than most of those among whom their father serves. After all, they can ask questions any time. They see close up how the gospel is at work in their father's life. They may often overhear his prayers for the spiritual welfare of his flock. They will see him pour himself out day and night to bless and not to burden them. They will see how his passion in the pulpit really is a reflection of his heartfelt passion for his people all the week long. And so, the responsibility to "improve" those privileges weighs heavily upon a pastor's child. "Everyone to whom much is given, from him much will be required" (Luke 12:48).

Yet all this notwithstanding, it's hard to find resources that offer real help. How shall a pastor's child navigate the failures of his pastor/father alongside the failures of the church his father pastors? When our instinct as sinners is usually to blame others ("The woman whom You gave to be with me, she gave me of the tree, and I ate" Gen. 3:12), how can we lead ministry children to see the sin festering in their own hearts when, as a matter of fact, the church often does bear at least some of the responsibility for their fathers' overwork and lack of availability? How can we help pastors' children believe and delight in the gospel and want to devote themselves to its advancement with zeal and urgency when in the apparent service of the gospel Dad is burning out? Certainly some of the solution must be to cultivate healthy pastors who are faithful fathers and loving husbands, who have inviolable boundaries that a church cannot transgress.

But no pastor gets the work/life balance right all the time. And for those difficult times a tool kit is needed to equip a minister's child to understand and integrate their father's weaknesses, the church's needs, their own sin and need of a savior, and the hope of the gospel. When a ministry child is raised in an environment of constant sacrifice, financial hardship, cultural dissonance, and unreasonable expectations, a clear view of the surpassing worth of Jesus Christ will be invaluable. We want our children to say, through tears perhaps, as they sacrifice along with the rest of the family, "Jesus is worth it! His gospel is worth it! The good of the church is worth it!" We want our children to join us on Christ's mission, with the same intrepid cheerfulness we ourselves must cultivate.

The aim of this volume is to provide many of the tools a pastor's child will need. But pastors and pastors' wives need to read it, too. Here are insights from seasoned preachers who have given years to the gospel ministry, from PKs who have wandered away but have come home to Christ in the end, from moms and dads who love their children and want them to thrive and want to help our children thrive, too. May the Lord use it to comfort troubled young hearts and direct them heavenward. May He use it to counsel troubled parents as they care for their ministry children. And above all, may Christ be magnified!

—David Strain

PART 1

LAYING THE FOUNDATION

IDENTITY CRISIS

1   PK or Child of the King?

Jasmine (Baucham) Holmes

Being a pastor presents myriad challenges. There are long days, late nights, unexpected complications…and that's just sermon preparation! Add the weight of shepherding the flock; bearing spiritual burdens; meeting unrealistic expectations; and fighting personal, cultural, and theological battles, and the challenges can be overwhelming.

However, the heaviest burden I bear as a pastor is recognizing and mitigating the toll pastoral ministry takes on my family, and especially on my children. My children did not volunteer for this duty; they were conscripted. Nor is there the remotest possibility of them opting out. As long as I serve, my children are PKs. And as long as my children are PKs, I am a shepherd of two flocks who must seek God's best for both. But as much as I love the church, and am committed to her health and well-being, "I have no greater joy than to hear that my children walk in truth" (3 John 1:4).

That is why reading this chapter, and what it represents, brings me unspeakable joy. Jasmine is our firstborn. As such, she has witnessed and endured more triumphs and trials than any of our other children. I am humbled by her wisdom, insight, candor, and spiritual maturity. More importantly, I am grateful for the grace God has shown her and the way He has used the crucible of growing up in the home of a pastor to shape her into a tool through which He gives help, hope, and healing to the body of Christ.

Warmly,
Voddie Baucham

Dear Pastor's Kid,

Hi, my name is Voddie's Daughter.

Certainly, that's not what's on my birth certificate, but it's the name I grew up hearing most often. "This is Voddie's Daughter," and, "Oh, wait, you're Voddie's Daughter?" and, "I can't believe you are Voddie's Daughter!"

My given name is Jasmine. And though many people don't take the time to learn it, the name is precious to me.

It wasn't always. When I was a kid, I bemoaned my floral name and thirsted after a handle with a bit more meaning. After all, it's *just* a flower—and not even a very good-smelling one at that! But, as I got older, I began to realize that, even if my name itself didn't have a very full meaning, I would come to give it the meaning that it lacked. When applied to me, Jasmine is not just a flower, but a girl with unique thoughts, feelings, gifts, callings, and aspirations. When it is applied to me, Jasmine is a deeply meaningful name, because it's a name attached to a person who has more meaning than any flower of the field.

And it's attached to a person who has more meaning than "just" that of a PK.

What is your name? And what does it mean? Not in the baby name book sense, but in the "Who are you?" sense. At twenty-seven years of age, I'm still figuring out my own personal answers to that question. Some of the defining factors are easier than others. I am Phillip's wife, Wynn's mama, and hopefully mama to a lot of other littles someday. I am a member of Redeemer Presbyterian Church, a teacher at St. Augustine School, and a writer. I am a friend and a mentor.

Some of the things are less visible and less important, but they're still important in the fabric of who I am. My favorite ice cream flavor (vanilla), my favorite color (any earth tone), my favorite movie from childhood (*The Princess Diaries*). What are your favorite things?

One thing that *is* a huge part of my identity, that belongs right up there after Phillip's wife and Wynn's mama, is that I am my father's daughter. But I also know that it isn't the *most* important thing about me.

Thank God for Your Dad

Don't get me wrong. I love my dad. For me as a homeschool student, he has been one of my favorite teachers, counselors, and confidants. We have myriad memories together, inside jokes, and well-worn conversational topics. He is my biggest advocate, my constant cheerleader, and my rock when the stresses of this life overwhelm me.

My dad was an amazing earthly example of God's fatherly love toward His children (1 John 1:3). He protected me (2 Thess. 3:3), he provided for me (Luke 12:24), he patiently instructed me (Ps. 25:12), and he led our family (Ps. 5:8). He did all of these things imperfectly, of course—God is the only perfect Father—but he did them with love, commitment, and diligence.

My dad is probably a little bit like your dad, in that he takes his responsibility as a father very seriously and loves me very much. One of my favorite stories illustrates this point in a hilarious way.

Back in the mid-2010s, body scanners were beginning to crop up in airports. When they were first launched, these scanners showed the human body in very intricate detail. Not only were they more invasive than metal detectors; some also believed that they violated our rights to privacy. My dad was one of these people.

We were on our way back from a trip to Atlanta, and my dad turned to his big family and said, "If they try to put you through the scanner, opt out." Now, we all knew that opting out meant a pretty invasive pat-down, and, in the grand scheme of things, it was a toss-up between whether we wanted airport security looking at our underwear or almost touching them. But, for my dad, it was the principle of the thing!

Back in those days, not everyone went through the body scanners. Customers would be randomly selected. Of course, yours truly was tapped and pulled out of the line.

Well, my dad hit the roof. He went on a patriotic speech about how we are American citizens and should not have to stand for such treatment! I will never forget the scene, or the way Dad hovered nearby during the pat-down to make sure I felt comfortable and safe.

I would be lying if I said that I wasn't a little bit embarrassed by all of the attention my dad's principles drew. But I would also be lying if I said I wasn't a little proud of him for standing up for me and doing his best to protect me.

And he really always has. From letting me sleep on his chest when I was just a tiny baby to trying his best to do my hair before school, from teaching me how to ride a bike or how to float in the swimming pool, from giving me advice in my friendships to being my confidant when I had crushes, from vetting my boyfriends to walking me down the aisle, from counseling me through the tough season after my son was born to being the jungle gym my little boy loves to climb.

Remember your dad's love for you. Recount the blessing of his faithfulness often. So many do not know the beauty of having a father who fears the Lord, and who takes his responsibility toward his children seriously (Eph. 6:1–4). Where your dad emulates your Father in heaven, encourage him and be encouraged! That is a gift! And it is not one that we should take for granted, although that can be so easy to do. But having a father who points you back to your Father in heaven is no small thing.

Thank God for Your Family

And because of that gift, there is part of me that doesn't mind being known as Voddie's Daughter, because that's a huge part of who I am. It would be foolish to pretend that my dad hasn't had a pivotal role in teaching and training me. You are your father's son or daughter, and that is a beautiful thing. You belong to a family that was put together by God for His glory, and that is an amazing gift.

In Ephesians 4, Paul begins talking about the local church, and how our relationships within the body can shape us for God's glory. He establishes the church as our primary source of Christian community, then brings his focus a bit narrower to talk about how the family is an even smaller community that we are blessed to be part of.

In chapter 5, he gives husbands the responsibility to love, lead, and disciple their wives (v. 25 and following). He charges them to be willing to sacrifice for them. He gives them the immense responsibility of cultivating a relationship with their wives that echoes the relationship between Christ and His church.

And he doesn't stop there. In Ephesians 6, he extends the responsibility for leading and guiding past the husband/wife relationship and into the parent/child relationship. He charges fathers to bring their children up "in the training and admonition of the Lord" (v. 4). This echoes the command that the Israelites were given in Deuteronomy, before entering the promised land:

> Hear, O Israel: The LORD our God, the LORD is one! You shall love the LORD your God with all your heart, with all your soul, and with all your strength.
>
> And these words which I command you today shall be in your heart. You shall teach them diligently to your children, and shall talk of them when you sit in your house, when you walk by the way, when you lie down, and when you rise up. You shall bind them as a sign on your hand, and they shall be as frontlets between your eyes. You shall write them on the doorposts of your house and your gates. (Deut. 6:4–9)

In this chapter, Moses gives the Israelites the incredible responsibility of cultivating family cultures that glorify and honor the Lord. What is your family culture like? What will you miss when you're gone, or what do you miss now that you've left?

When I got married, I missed my family's culture much more than I anticipated. One of my favorite parts of it was gathering around the breakfast table every morning to recite the catechism.

"Who made you?" my mom or dad used to ask.

"God!" my brother and I used to clamor, but as we grew into adulthood we listened to our younger siblings.

"What else did God make?"

"God made all things!"

"Why did God make you and all things?"

"For His own glory!"

Breakfast seemed so quiet when I left! It was just me and my husband, and I missed those sweet little voices being discipled by my parents. And I missed being one of those little voices, too!

My parents understood their responsibility to disciple us and raise us in the discipline and instruction of God. I am so grateful for that! If your parents understand this, it's no small thing. Their obedience is an immense blessing to you.

Thank God You're an Arrow

But God did not create us to be born, to live, and to die in the exact same families that we started out in. In fact, one of the major purposes of being raised in a Christian family is to live out a legacy of godliness in our own homes.

Back in Ephesians 5, we read, "For this reason a man shall leave his father and mother and be joined to his wife, and the two shall become one flesh" (v. 31). So mothers and fathers raise their children in the nurture and admonition of the Lord, then those children grow up and get married and raise more children in the nurture and admonition of the Lord…and that's how we establish a godly legacy. In fact, even if these adult children never get married, they still grow up and proclaim the gospel to others (Matt. 28:16–20) and have "spiritual children" whom they teach and train for God's glory.

In Proverbs, Solomon tells us that children are like arrows in the hands of a mighty warrior (Ps. 127:4). Arrows do a warrior no good if they stay in his pack; they are made to be launched in battle. Similarly, pastors' kids aren't made to sit in their parents' shadows for the rest of their lives; they are made to be launched from their homes and into a hurting world after having been trained to bring the good news of Christ Jesus.

So, all of that teaching and training that your parents are pouring into you are ultimately being poured for God's glory—not their own. For me, this has been beautifully illustrated by my marriage to my husband. I lived at home with my family until I was twenty-four. Even though I was working, in grad school, and doing "my own thing" a lot of the time, much of my daily life still revolved around the Baucham flow. I helped my mom around the house, helped homeschool my siblings, worked in my dad's ministry in different capacities, and was an active member of our church.

There were definitely challenges to being an adult daughter living at home. I have a wonderful relationship with both of my parents, but that didn't stop us from occasionally butting heads. I love my siblings like crazy, but that didn't stop me from getting annoyed with them some-times. And I loved my family dynamic very much, but that didn't stop me from yearning for a little independence.

When my husband came, I got just what I was asking for. After a few months of marriage, the two of us moved to Minneapolis, Minnesota, away from my family, friends, and everything familiar to me back in Houston, Texas. And my own family moved to Lusaka, Zambia, an entire continent away.

Suddenly, even though people who followed my dad's ministry still knew me as "Voddie's Daughter," I was not living my life primarily as her anymore. And when my husband and I moved back to his home-town in Mississippi, I went from being known as "Voddie's Daughter" to being "Phillip's wife." The Baucham family culture started giving way to our Holmes family culture. Things I thought were true of me started to morph and change outside the herd mentality that often comes with a family name. Phillip and I developed our own way of relating to one another, our own way of doing life together. And we are still working on it, especially since we're only three years in.

How are you different from your family? How has the Lord been shaping your unique identity? Whether it be through taking a mission trip, going to college, getting married, having kids, or just taking your first job, jumping into ministry opportunities, or cultivating new hob-bies, the ways that you branch off from your family tree can be beautiful expressions of the unique calling that God has given *you*.

You are not to be taught to glorify God so that you bring honor to your family name. That is a secondary benefit, certainly. I do hope to make my parents proud in the things that I accomplish. Since they brought me up in the ways of the Lord, and since my heart desires noth-ing more than to honor that God, the things that I am pursuing so often line up with the things my parents would have me pursue! If you have godly parents with godly priorities, you might find that the same will remain true of you. Praise God for that! It is such a gift.

But that gift of pleasing our parents is not our goal. Our goal is to bring honor to our King. This will help us keep our priorities straight even in those moments when we *do* disappoint our parents and don't meet their expectations for us by following what we believe God expects us to do. For some of us, that will be a rarity—an anomaly. But it is something we must be willing to do in pursuit of peace with our ultimate Family.

Thank God the Story Is Bigger than Your Family

And that's the most beautiful part of the story.

Families were not made to revolve around the father, bringing glory and honor to him, but, rather, to revolve around the Lord. They were not made to be little islands isolated from the rest of the world but, rather, an integral part of Christian communities made to impact the world. Children are not born to remain in the same family unit until the day they die, but to carry forth the faith of that family unit into both physical and spiritual families to the glory and honor of God.

This thing is so much bigger than being So-and-So's daughter or son; it's about being the daughter or son of our heavenly Father.

This is good news for kids who are born into less-than-ideal family circumstances. Even if your father is not a man of God, or your mother is not walking with the Lord, you are not defined by that dysfunctional family dynamic. You are defined by the more inclusive family that supersedes your earthly home. You are defined by the family of faith.

You see, the first family ever created was incredibly dysfunctional. Adam and Eve sinned against God by directly disobeying His command (Gen. 3:3), and they brought sin into this world. The sin even impacted their own family—one of their sons killed another son (4:8). The dysfunction didn't stop there. The world grew so full of sin in the following generations that God wiped it out with a great flood (6:17), saving only one family. And even *that* family struggled with sins like drunkenness and a son's mockery (8:13–22).

Then, God made a covenant with one of Noah's descendants, Abraham (Gen. 17:9). But Abraham wasn't perfect either—he was a liar (20:2). And so was his son Isaac (26:7), and so was Isaac's son Jacob (27:19). Jacob's sons were so dysfunctional and jealous that they sold their own brother into slavery (37:18–36). And, many, many years and many, many dysfunctional family members later, even David, a man after God's own heart (1 Sam. 13:14), turned out to be an adulterer and a murderer (2 Samuel 11).

This family tree is full of people who disobey God's law, and, as such, are worthy of death, hell, and the grave—because we all are (Rom. 3:23). We are all born into sin (Ps. 51:5). But Abraham, Isaac, and Jacob's family tree has a very important member: Jesus Christ. And He came to live the perfect life that none of His ancestors could live, because He was God wrapped in flesh (John 10:30). Not only did Christ live a perfect life, but God "made Him who knew no sin to be sin for us, that we might become the righteousness of God" (2 Cor. 5:21).

The story is bigger than Adam and Eve's family. And we should be grateful for that, because Adam and Eve's family is full of wretched sinners who could not live up to God's standard. The story revolves not around our individual families but around the pivotal member of Adam's: Jesus Christ. He trumps the most dysfunctional families on the planet by bringing us into His family, and He supersedes the most righteous families on the planet by outshining every last one of them.

Your family is not the beginning and end of the story—Christ is. So being So-and-So's daughter or So-and-So's son pales in comparison to whether or not you belong to our Savior. Earthly families will pass away, but Christ's family remains.

Thank God Your Identity Is in Christ

None of our families can live up to the righteous standard of the Most High God. Not a single one of them. And none of our families can be as terrible as some of the members that God saw fit to include in Jesus's earthly family tree.

What does this say to us? It says that the most important part of who you are isn't your last name or your dad's position. Nor is the most important part of you what you make of yourself. It says that the most important part of who you are is whether or not you are found in Christ.

Do you know God? Have you believed in your heart and confessed with your mouth that Jesus Christ is Lord (Rom. 10:9)? If you haven't, I urge you to do so. Put down this book and turn to Christ. Put down this book and seek the transformational truth of His Word.

If you have, then you are part of the family of faith, which is so much more important than the pastor's kid title that you wear. If you have, *your name*, not your dad's name or your mom's name, but *your name*, is written down in the Lamb's Book of Life (Rev. 3:5). If you have, then it doesn't matter who your dad is, or what your dad does, because your most important Father is in heaven. If you have, it doesn't matter how you disappoint your earthly father (and we all disappoint our earthly parents from time to time); when God looks at us, He sees His Son, with whom He is *completely* satisfied (Matt. 3:17). And we are being conformed to the image of that Son daily (Rom. 8:29).

That is the good news about families! Not that your dad is a man of God, or that your mom is a superwoman (as I think nearly all pastors' wives are). Not that you were raised in a godly home or that your parents did mostly everything right. No. Those things are good news only because of *the* Good News: that Christ died on the cross to reconcile us to God, and to craft a family that supersedes all earthly molds, even as it includes those who do follow God.

It's the same good news for the pastors' kids with amazing fathers and the pastors' kids with lackluster dads, for the moments when those amazing dads are being amazing and those moments when even the most amazing dads fail us; we have a Father in heaven who loves us perfectly, and who loves our earthly fathers perfectly. Fathers, mothers, daughters, sons, we all need the same Savior to intercede for us. And that's the family name we should be proclaiming.

Thank God for the Opportunity to Remind Others

When I announced that I was going to have a son, we got so many excited congratulations from so many wonderful people! Everyone was so excited, especially me, because I had had a sneaking suspicion that I was just made to be a boy mom.

But more than one person asked me if I would be naming my son "Voddie Junior." I was furious. I knew that it was most likely a joke, but the joke angered me. If my son were going to be named after *anyone* in my family, it was going to be *his* dad, not mine! I made a post about it on social media and tried to inform everyone (as politely as I could) that it was very disrespectful to my husband to congratulate my dad and not him, and to insinuate that the Baucham family name needed to live on in this Holmes family household.

I was so encouraged by the overwhelmingly positive responses to the boundaries that I set. Pastors' kids thanked me for speaking up; pastors applauded me for putting my husband first; my own mother nodded her emphatic approval, and so did my dad.

My parents both understood that in order for me to have the same godly marriage that they had, I was going to have to learn how to put my husband first, even (and sometimes especially) when it came to my family of origin, whom I love very much.

As you grow up, there will be moments when you just smile and nod when someone mistakenly thinks that your identity is wrapped up in your being So-and-So's daughter or So-and-So's son, because, inwardly, you will know the truth. But there will also be moments when you know it's time to speak up to remind others (and yourself!) that you are a separate person with a separate identity that is tied into being the daughter or son of another Father entirely.

You'll learn when the right time is to do both of those things. In the meantime, though, I hope that this letter encourages you to plant your identity firmly in Christ, digging your roots deeper and deeper every day by saturating yourself in the truth of His Word and the fullness of the community that He has given you, both in your nuclear family and in the family of the church.

It's a balancing act, definitely, and sometimes you'll teeter too far over toward one side: some days, you'll be a bit too eager to throw off your earthly family's name, too primed for independence to appreciate your parents; some days, you'll be a bit too complacent to forge your own path, too afraid to follow the Lord wherever He leads. God's grace is sufficient for both kinds of days, and I pray that He will see you through each and every one of them as you find out more and more of who you are in Him.

Your fellow PK,
Jasmine

Jasmine Holmes is a wife, mom, speaker, and the author of *Mother to Son: Letters to a Black Boy on Identity and Hope*. She and her husband, Phillip, have two sons, and they are members of Redeemer Church in Jackson, Mississippi.

EXPECTATIONS
Who Sets the Standard?

Megan (Evans) Hill

Megan was born and raised a pastor's kid. She gets it. Really. She's glad to have been a PK. She sees the Lord's good hand in her upbringing. She also knows that being a PK can feel weird at times. PKs feel pressure to be some kind of "special" Christian when really all they want, at their best, is to be a "mere" Christian. Megan has lived through all this so she can write about it with sympathy and skill. In fact, she even has PKs of her own these days. Savor her words. You just might find a kindred spirit.

Warmly,
Brad and Patsy Evans

Dear Pastor's Kid,

Just a few weeks ago, my boys came out of Sunday school with frustration on their faces. "Mom!" they said. "It's so hard to be the pastor's kids. If the teacher asks a question, and we get the right answer, the other kids say, 'Well, you just knew that because you're the pastor's kid.' But if the teacher asks something and we get it wrong, the kids say, 'Ooooh! You should have known that. You're the pastor's kid!'"

I understood exactly what my children were talking about because my dad is a pastor, too. When I was younger, my friends at church and school also dismissed my right answers and triumphantly pounced on my wrong ones. Sometimes, they questioned my choices about what movies to watch, what clothes to wear, or what jokes to tell. ("Are you allowed to do that?" they would ask. "Does your dad know about that?") Adults, too, had things to say about my position as their pastor's kid.

"You are a perfect pastor's daughter!" they would smile when I dressed up and accompanied my dad on visits to the nursing home. Or they would whisper to newcomers, "She's the pastor's kid," when I helped with VBS or received public recognition for my catechism memory.

The comments you hear might be slightly different. People might give their thoughts about your haircut, your hobbies, or your habit of biting your fingernails. People might express their surprise that you're afraid of speaking in public (unlike your dad) or that you've never heard of a certain theologian (whom your dad apparently loves). People might assume that you will be their child's best friend. People might even embarrass you by always introducing you to others as "our pastor's amazing son."

Each of these remarks—whether intended to be encouraging or cautionary—reveals that other people often have opinions about what a pastor's kid should be like. In other words, people in your church and community have *expectations*.

In this letter, I'd like to discuss how a pastor's kid (you!) can understand and respond to other people's expectations. Obviously, your highest goal is to bring glory to God in the place where He has put you, and His Word gives helpful direction about how you can do that as a pastor's kid. First, we will look at whether it is fair for people to have expectations of you. Next, we'll talk about situations in which people's expectations might actually be an act of God's mercy toward you. And, finally, we'll consider how you can respond to expectations in a way that is a blessing to those around you.

That's Not Fair! Or Is It?

Since so many of the comments you receive have the term "pastor's kid" attached to them, it can feel like you—and your siblings—are being singled out for expectations. After all, nobody else in the church (except your siblings, if you have them) has to live up to being the child of the pastor. And that doesn't seem quite fair.

But before you begin to feel frustrated and mistreated, let me remind you that there are some relationships in your life where expectations are entirely fair.

In the first place, it is fair for God to have expectations of you. When you were younger, you may have memorized the catechism question and answer that reads, "Why should you glorify God? Because he made me and takes care of me." That's a simple answer written for little kids, but it is true for everyone. God is the One who created us and who provides for all of our needs; He has the right to expect we would live in a way that glorifies Him. God's expectations are also the most important expectations in our lives; any other expectations from any other source should follow from God's expectations and be consistent with them.

God tells us His expectations in His Word, and He reminds us of them by His Spirit. For example, God expects you to sing with your whole heart in worship (Ps. 98:4). God expects you to pray regularly (1 Thess. 5:16–18). God expects you to listen and learn from His Word as it is read and preached (1 Thess. 2:13). God expects you to serve others (1 Peter 4:10). God expects you to become more like His Son, the Lord Jesus Christ (Rom. 13:14).

The good news is that God does not simply lay out expectations for you. He also gives you the power to fulfill those expectations. If you belong to Christ, you are no longer under the threat of God's wrath and no longer in bondage to sin. Christ fully satisfied God's expectations on your behalf. And, by His Holy Spirit, He is even now making you holy, just as He is holy. You strive to fulfill God's expectations in the power of the Spirit and out of love for Christ.

And there are also others in your life whom God has given the right to expect things of you. Under God, your parents, the elders of your church, and your fellow church members can all legitimately expect that you will avail yourself of the help of the Spirit and seek to grow in Christlikeness.

Your parents and church elders have a unique relationship to you as those who have God-given authority over you. It is their responsibility to teach you God's Word, to set an example of godliness for you to follow, and to shepherd your soul by instructing you. They do this as those who "must give account" to God for fulfilling their responsibilities toward you (Heb. 13:17). The verse goes on to say that you, in turn, receive their instruction "with joy and not with grief" because they are exercising authority for your spiritual good. This means that whether their expectations are major (you should participate in all the meetings of the church) or comparatively minor (you should dress in a certain way), you can submit cheerfully, knowing that God promises it will "be well with you" when you obey "in the Lord" (Deut. 5:16; Eph. 6:1–2).

As authorities, your parents and elders also help you to establish priorities for your life. With so many expectations coming at you from so many directions, it can sometimes be difficult to sort out which things are important. Mrs. Smith thinks you should volunteer for the nursery. Mr. Jones thinks you should play guitar for the youth group. Miss Adams thinks everyone else should stop asking you to do things. Having the good gift of parents and elders means that you have wise people to direct you. Don't be shy about asking them for counsel and freely submitting to their advice.

Finally, other church members have a right to expect things of you. If you've ever joined a sports team (or a robotics club or a drama group), you know that team members have expectations of one another. Your teammates probably expected you to play by the rules—run to first base before you run to second base, for example. They probably also expected that you would show up and participate to your best ability. They might even have made direct suggestions: "try it this way" or "don't do that so much." Why do they do this? They want the team to do well.

The church is much like a team. The New Testament calls it a body, and the idea is similar: "Speaking the truth in love, [you] may grow up in all things into Him who is the head—Christ—from whom the whole body, joined and knit together by what every joint supplies, according to the effective working by which every part does its share, causes growth of the body for the edifying of itself in love" (Eph. 4:15–16).

All the parts of a body work together for a common goal (v. 16), and if one part is not working well, the whole body suffers. When people in your church make suggestions about what you should do or not do, it is helpful to remember that you and they are on the same team, part of the same body. This means that you all want the same thing—a healthy body that matches Christ, its perfect head (v. 15)—and that your well-being is connected to everyone else's well-being. Many of the expectations of people in your church constitute "the truth in love" (v. 15) for your spiritual growth. Your fellow church members want you to become more like Christ so the whole church will be more like Christ.

When I was growing up, I was expected to take an interest in the people in my church. When they spoke to me, I knew I should speak to them and use their names. When they needed someone to open a heavy door or pick up a child from the nursery, I knew I should offer to help. Whenever I could, I knew it was a good idea to visit church members in the hospital or nursing home with my dad. On some special occasions, I would even stand at the back of the church and shake hands alongside my dad after a church service.

Those expectations were big, but they weren't unfair. In the first place, God Himself commands, "Let each of you look out not only for his own interests, but also for the interests of others" (Phil. 2:4). In the second place, this expected service was my job as a part of the church team. By doing those things, I grew in Christlikeness and encouraged others to do the same.

While your first response to expectations might be "That's not fair!" it is helpful to remember that God Himself has placed certain people in your life whose expectations He wants you to heed.

That's Not Kind! Or Is It?

But what about times when other people are trying to correct you or change your behavior? Picture this: You are just about to do something that seems really fun. Maybe you are talking with your friends, making plans to go to a movie or a concert. Maybe you are about to play a prank on your youth group leader. Maybe you are using all your charms to convince a church kitchen volunteer to let you (and your friends) have an extra slice of that chocolate cake. And then it happens. Someone frowns at you and tells you not to.

Even though those situations are uncomfortable—and might make you wish everyone in the church would stop looking at you all the time—they can actually be God's mercy to you. Scripture tells us about two Old Testament pastor's kids who received lots of head shaking from the people in God's covenant community. Hophni and Phinehas were the children of the high priest, Eli. And they did not pay any attention to the warnings they got from God's people:

> Now the sons of Eli were corrupt; they did not know the LORD.
> And the priests' custom with the people was that when any man

offered a sacrifice, the priest's servant would come with a three-pronged fleshhook in his hand while the meat was boiling. Then he would thrust it into the pan, or kettle, or caldron, or pot; and the priest would take for himself all that the fleshhook brought up. So they did in Shiloh to all the Israelites who came there. Also, before they burned the fat, the priest's servant would come and say to the man who sacrificed, "Give meat for roasting to the priest, for he will not take boiled meat from you, but raw."

And if the man said to him, "They should really burn the fat first; then you may take as much as your heart desires," he would then answer him, "No, but you must give it now; and if not, I will take it by force."

Therefore the sin of the young men was very great before the LORD, for men abhorred the offering of the LORD. (1 Sam. 2:12–17)

In the book of Leviticus, God made generous and specific provision for His priests. When God's people brought Him offerings, the priest's family always received "the breast of the wave offering and the thigh of the heave offering" (Lev. 7:34) as their portion. But Hophni and Phinehas were not content with those pieces of meat, and they made their own rules. At first, they would stick a fork in the pot and take whatever they could grab. Even worse, they began demanding a piece of the raw meat before it was offered, robbing God of the burned fat that was His due.

God's people were rightly bothered. They knew what God's expectations were, and they expected Eli's sons to obey. They first warned Hophni and Phinehas directly (1 Sam. 2:16), and, later, they took their complaints to Eli, who reported back to his sons (vv. 22–24). But these pastor's kids refused to take to heart the head-shaking of God's people. Maybe they had convinced themselves that everyone was being too picky. Maybe they thought God's people were expecting too much of them. Certainly, they loved their sin more than they loved God's glory. And they died because of it (v. 25).

How different it might have been for Hophni and Phinehas if they had taken people's expectations seriously! Though those pastor's kids didn't want to believe it, the frowning congregational members were actually a provision of God's mercy. God's people were trying to help Eli's sons see and repent of their sin. For you, too, people's head-shaking and eyebrow-lifting can be a blessing. Like Hophni and Phinehas, unless you recognize your sin, you will not confess it. Unless you confess your sin and repent of it, you will not find forgiveness. And unless you find forgiveness, you cannot enjoy fellowship with God.

In my life, I've been corrected by church members for running in the hallways, helping myself to drinks from the church refrigerator, making too much noise in the back row during a service, and failing to include church visitors in my group of friends. At the time, those frowns didn't always seem like much of a blessing, but I eventually realized they were God's mercy to me. God was not allowing me to continue in sin. He loved me enough to send someone to stop me by "speaking the truth in love" (Eph. 4:15).

The next time you encounter a frowning church member, ask yourself, "Could this actually be an act of God's kindness?"

I Can't Do Anything Right! Or Can I?

In other situations, however, people might have wrong or misplaced expectations of you. They might assume that you will be rebellious simply because they have known other rebellious pastors' kids. Or they might expect you to have specific spiritual gifts or to know a certain number of Bible verses or catechism answers. If they are older or from a different culture, they might have expectations about how you will act in church situations based on the way pastors' kids were expected to act during their own childhood. Other people might even expect you to form an exclusive relationship with their family and be hurt when you are friendly but not best friends. As we will see, these faulty expectations are an opportunity to live up to a different standard—God's standard—and to encourage the church in the process.

The Bible tells us about another pastor's kid. His name was Timothy. Timothy was not a pastor's kid in a biological sense; it seems likely that his father was not even a Christian (2 Tim. 1:5). But the great pastor Paul mentored Timothy and publicly called him his child (1 Tim. 1:2; 2 Tim. 1:2). People in the New Testament churches would have thought of Timothy as the pastor's kid. And so Paul gave this instruction to him: "Let no one despise your youth, but be an example to the believers in word, in conduct, in love, in spirit, in faith, in purity" (1 Tim. 4:12).

First, Paul acknowledged that Timothy would likely face some misguided expectations from God's people: "Let no one despise your youth." Because Timothy was a young man in a position of authority in the church, people might have looked down on him because he wasn't very old. They might have assumed that a young pastor's kid couldn't possibly have the necessary wisdom to lead Christ's church. They might have assumed that he would fall into the same sins that other young people are tempted to. They might have expected him to speak or act in a certain way (perhaps just like his "father," Paul) and then blame his age when he didn't. But Paul didn't want Timothy to be discouraged. Timothy was the age he was, in the position he was in, because the sovereign God had placed him there. You can take comfort from this, too. You are the person you are, in the position you are in, because God has put you there. Don't be overly bothered by people's wrong expectations.

As I already mentioned, your parents and elders can help you decide which expectations are valid and which are mistaken. Just as Paul told his "son," Timothy, that expectations related to his age shouldn't be a concern for him, those who have authority in your life can tell you which expectations you should respectfully dismiss.

Next, Paul encouraged Timothy. He shouldn't be paralyzed by faulty expectations, but instead he should turn them into an opportunity to be a blessing in the church. He put it this way: "Let no one despise your youth, but be an example to the believers in word, in conduct, in love, in spirit, in faith, in purity" (1 Tim. 4:12). Instead of people shaking their heads at your failure to live up to *their* expectations, they should be able to give thanks for how well you strive to live up to *God's* expectations. Paul gives priorities for the pastor's kid that describe an entire life of holiness, focused on the things God says in this verse are most important.

We talked earlier about how the church is a body that depends on every part. Setting an example of godliness is a way you can make a valuable contribution to the health of your church. Not only are you not the broken arm or rumbling stomach—causing the whole body to function weakly—you are actually an important part of encouraging the whole body's Christlikeness. When you live by God's perfect expectations, you will bless everyone around you. People who observe you will gain a fresh vision for what the Spirit can do in someone's life.

Who wouldn't give thanks to God for a pastor's kid who practices godly speech and actions, relates to others with love and purity, and takes her faith seriously?

So, when you face expectations (and I'm sure you will), I hope you will remember the three things we discussed:

- Expectations that come from someone—God, a parent, an elder, or a church member—who has a right to expect things from you should be taken seriously.

- Expectations that discourage you from sinning are God's kind mercy toward you.

- Expectations that are misguided are an opportunity to refocus on the priorities that God sets for your life.

I'd like to close this letter with a reminder of something you already read in chapter 1. In that letter, Jasmine Holmes wrote to you about your identity as a pastor's kid and told you that your worth before God has nothing to do with your role as the son or daughter of a pastor and everything to do with your adoption as the son or daughter of God. Remember this truth—that Christ purchased you with His own blood, dressed you in His righteousness, gives you His Spirit, and never stops praying for you—even and especially when you feel overwhelmed by expectations. And be encouraged! No sin or ignorance, no task done or undone, no well-meaning church member or teasing Sunday school classmate can ever separate you from the love of God in Christ Jesus.

Being a pastor's kid is not an easy role, but it is exactly the role that God has chosen for you. I am confident that He will use even people's expectations to conform you to the image of His Son. And I hope that you will learn to love Him more as He works in you.

Your fellow pastor's kid,

Megan Hill

Megan Hill is a pastor's wife and a pastor's daughter. She is the author of three books: *A Place to Belong: Learning to Love the Local Church*; *Contentment: Seeing God's Goodness*; and *Praying Together: The Priority and Privilege of Prayer: In Our Homes, Communities, and Churches*. She also serves as an editor for the Gospel Coalition. She lives in Massachusetts with her husband and four children, where they belong to West Springfield Covenant Community Church (PCA).

COUNT YOUR BLESSINGS
Enjoying the Benefits of Being a PK

Joel and Mary Beeke

While my sisters and I were growing up, my parents, Joel and Mary Beeke, were very "normal." We enjoyed family time, education, and vacations together. This normal life also involved Dad visiting people at all hours of the day, working late into the night on sermons, and attending lots of funerals, weddings, and events. This intensely busy life obviously had its positives and negatives, but it was the only world I knew, and I enjoyed it. As I grew up I realized the challenges, responsibilities, and opportunities of being in a pastor's family.

As I became a teenager, my dad's ministry scaled upward from pastoring a large church to writing many influential books and helping to found and expand the Puritan Reformed Theological Seminary. With assistant pastors taking over many of the church labors, Dad was able to focus on speaking worldwide, authoring many titles, and training men for ministry and seminary leadership in other countries. My mom actively worked alongside him, leading the Ministry Wives Fellowship, speaking internationally, and writing a best-selling book, *The Law of Kindness*.

My dad led us consistently in family worship. He often spoke to us of spiritual, deep matters. One recurring theme was leadership. By example, he was incredibly diligent and efficient in his work. As I founded a business, he guided me, and I sought to implement what I had observed for two decades. My mom did almost too much for others. Thinking of herself was never an option. She urged us to always ask "What's next?" in chores and in service to God and others. Her tears always come quickly and from the heart, whether because of a prayer need or a moment of joy in someone else's blessing.

Ultimately, it should be said that both of my parents have an intense passion for reaching every heart in this world with the Reformed experiential truths of God's Word. God has used their ministry in seminary, church, and authorship to incredible ends that none of us could have ever envisioned.

Your Fellow PK,
Calvin Beeke

Dear Pastor's Kid,

You are chosen—chosen by God to be a preacher's kid, a PK. That is who you are. But you are more than that. You are first and foremost a valuable human being created by God in His image. We hope and pray that you are born again, that you are a child of the King. You are unique in your personality, in your likes and dislikes, in your appearance, and in your life experiences. We don't know you personally, but we have a son and two daughters who are PKs, and we know hundreds of other PKs, so we would like to share some thoughts with you on the subject.

In a word, you are blessed. You have many privileges that others don't have. But before we go into detail, we realize that some of you might not see it this way. You struggle with being a PK. Toward the end of this chapter, we address some of the burdens you might be grappling with. If this is you, please read that section first, then come back to the blessings.

We also need to clear the air about stereotypes of PKs. You know—your reputation of being rebellious because everybody is watching you. People expect the minister's kids to behave better than other church kids, but you are going to prove to them that you can be as wild and bad as the rest. That is an unfair judgment. (We certainly hope you are not proving it true!) You are made for greater and loftier things. Let's abolish that stereotype. We challenge you to rise to the circumstances around you, to see the opportunities before you, and to live the full and exciting life that awaits you.

The Blessings

Significance

Every dad has an occupation, a calling. But there is something unique about your dad's calling as a minister. He deals with matters of life and death, of heaven and hell, and of body and soul. There is real significance to your dad's occupation. Every type of honest labor is important and honored by God. But in a sense, your dad is on the front lines of a battle—the battle between good and evil. God's sacred calling is on your dad. He is enlisted in the army of King Jesus. He has a high calling, yet he must remain a humble servant. He is a representative of God to His church.

Action is all around you in your church, and you have a front-row seat. Your love, prayers, and walk with God are a great encouragement to your dad as he serves the Lord. You are part of the team that holds up his hands. Your parents love you, and you are loved, cared for, and prayed over by the congregation. You have significance. Your life matters.

Adventure

The most exciting thing that can ever happen is for sinners to be saved by grace. When the power of the Holy Spirit washes their sins away and changes their lives from darkness to light, you get to see this happening! You also get to witness the joy of couples falling in love and getting married, the birth of babies, and all the other milestones of life. Yes, there are the sad times, too—disease, broken relationships, disappointments, and death. But God's Word is our road map, a light on our path and a guide for our feet to help us through. Jesus Christ is our solid ground, and we, as a church family, grow stronger and closer to Him by going through the hard times, though they may leave scars.

If you are a missionary kid, you have the additional adventure of living in a foreign culture, along with its challenges—less than ideal living conditions, insects and reptiles, cultural conundrums, and a strange language. But it wouldn't be an adventure if there weren't challenges, after all. Your experiences are shaping you, and who can tell how God will use you?

You get to experience vicariously the adventures of those who sit around your dinner table and tell their stories: Pastor W., who was addicted, homeless, and violent, but God snatched him from self-destruction and is using his intense energy to shepherd sheep in Ohio; Rev. K., who faced down the cannibals in Irian Jaya and later saw them come to Christ; Dr. H., who has been persecuted numerous times for bringing the gospel to dangerous parts of Africa. You know Christianity is not for wimps! And you know God is real.

God's Presence

You have witnessed life lived in the presence of God. There is something about the ministry that keeps your dad and mom needy and dependent on God. Our dads were not ministers, but they were ruling elders in the church for decades, so we almost felt like we were PKs. And we had the privilege of seeing them walk in God's presence. My (Mary's) dad's comprehensive integrity—at home, church, and work—left a blessed impression on me.

You, too, are blessed to be witnesses of that and, in many cases, participants in it. So much of everyday life naturally revolves around God in your family—talking about Him in family worship, in daily life, and with visitors; praying often in the family for one another and for others in need, whether they are present or absent; going to church services and participating in a variety of church activities; living consciously in the fear of God, so that you value the smiles and frowns of God more than the smiles and frowns of people.

We trust you have witnessed in your own family what many children never witness—that life is to be lived, as the sixteenth-century Reformers put it, *coram Deo*—that is, before the face or presence of God. That is one of life's greatest blessings.

Prayer

Your life has been bathed with prayer. How can you overestimate that privilege? We are really blessed, because both our parents were mentors for us in this critical area of life. When I (Joel) was nine years old, my dad, who was a dedicated ruling elder in the church for forty years, asked me this unforgettable question: "Son, do you know what the biggest difference is between a believer and an unbeliever?" His answer was, "A believer always has a place to go: the open throne of grace." And then he added, "I wish I could write this with an iron pen on your heart"—and he did, because I never forgot it. Then he said, "Never forget that the freedom to pray is worth more than anything this world can offer you." How true that is!

Think about it—you've had a double measure of this blessing as a PK. Many people in the church have been praying for you from before you were born. They love your parents, and they love you as part of their pastor's family. They sincerely care about you—enough to pray for you weekly and perhaps in some cases daily. Wow—what a blessing! John Newton, famous for writing "Amazing Grace," said that one of his greatest blessings and encouragements was that he believed that at nearly any moment of his life someone was lifting up his name before his Father in heaven. People who pray for you really are your best friends. You have a heavy dose of blessing in this area.

Then, too, you are being raised in a home where it is as natural to pray as it is to breathe. You've probably heard your parents pray for you wholeheartedly and earnestly hundreds of times—something that many children, including some children of church members, seldom or perhaps even never experience. Moreover, your parents have been hospitable, so that many visitors have graced your home with sincere prayers for you as well. We would venture to say that the prayers offered for you by your parents, church members, and visitors in themselves more than make up for all the disadvantages of being a PK. Thank God every day for those who remember you in prayer.

Family Worship
Your life has been shaped by the inestimable blessing of daily, godly family worship. Your father, together with your mother, has taught you from the Bible every day, probably with great diligence and ability. When my (Joel's) parents had their fiftieth wedding anniversary, all five of us children agreed to thank each of them for one thing without speaking to our siblings ahead of time. And all five of us thanked my dad for his Sunday evening family worship, which had a particular focus on his teaching us about the Lord's saving work as evidenced in John Bunyan's *Pilgrim's Progress*.

When our own firstborn got married, it was humbling to hear that his first thank-you to us in his closing remarks was for teaching him daily from God's Word in family worship. Participating in family worship in a pastor's home every day is an inestimable privilege that prepares you for life. It gives you an example and a head start for establishing your own home one day, so that you, too, can bathe your home in prayer. One of the old Puritans used to say that a prayerful family is like a little church, but a prayerless family is like a home without a roof, exposed to all the storms of heaven.

Love and Self-Sacrifice

Because you have been raised in a pastor's family, your life has probably been graced with the need for love, teamwork, and self-sacrifice. Blessed are you if your parents are deeply in love with each other and you have witnessed and experienced that love in action all your life through their affection, their kind words, and their self-sacrificing spirit in Christ Jesus to each other and to you.

That, too, is worth more than any disadvantage you might feel about being a PK. That loving, sacrificial spirit has also rubbed off on you, we trust, in teaching you the importance of teamwork and kindness in the home, for Christ's sake.

Wisdom

Your life is blessed with parents whom you may approach for wise, biblical advice on nearly any subject under the sun. Many Christian young people have Christian parents, but they find it difficult to ask them for advice because their parents are not gifted with much wisdom. If the parents do have wisdom, they may find it difficult to put it into words. Treasure the storehouse of advice you can receive from your parents, who have much experience in advising all kinds of people about all kinds of problems from the Word of God.

Handling Trials

You have more experience than most of your peers at witnessing how life's trials should be handled. With your dad in the ministry, you have had a chance to see his and your mother's maturity in handling criticism and challenges in the church. You have seen suffering at close hand with people your parents dearly love in the church who are diagnosed with cancer or have other diseases or afflictions. In the joys of life, like marriages and new babies, and in troubles and trials—the real stuff of life and how to respond to it—you have had more experience than your peers to mature you and prepare you for the real world.

Probably you've seen your parents needy, and you've heard them crying out to God for help and wisdom; such things can make invaluable impressions on you. The way your parents handle trials can be like an open book of wisdom for you.

Service
We all dream of greatness, especially when we're young. Whatever our talents are—sports, mechanics, design, business—we want to excel. We also want others to think highly of us, and we want to be loved by someone special whom we also love. That is all normal and wonderful.

But the greatest greatness is described in Luke 22:26 (KJV): "He that is greatest among you, let him be as the younger; and he that is chief, as he that doth serve." Serving others is the only real path to greatness. I've seen that for many decades in my (Mary's) mother's life—in fact, it seemed that nearly all her life was devoted to serving other people. Our parents' lives of service have left indelible marks on us.

As a PK, you have more opportunity to serve than your peers might have. You see up front and close who is having emotional or relationship or health troubles. You know who "the least of these my brethren" are. You know whom to give a cup of cold water to. You know whom to visit and whom to feed. You are able to develop empathy for those who are suffering.

What are your gifts? Welcoming someone new? It means a lot more to the new kid in church if *you* include him than if an adult welcomes him. Does that quiet girl look extra sad today? Chat with her and draw her out. Are you a strong leader? Stand up for the guy or girl who is picked on.

Your dad is God's servant, but as a young person you are better equipped for reaching your peers on an eye-to-eye level. Don't infiltrate them with bad behavior, but permeate them with kindness and serving. You are needed and valuable in the church. Use every opportunity to help others, and you will find yourself richer for it. Your dad is God's ordained servant who ministers with joy. Why shouldn't you be God's unordained servant who ministers with joy?

Opportunities

You generally have more opportunities to reach out to others beyond your peer group than most kids your age. You have more opportunities to visit with adults than they do, due to the many visitors you receive in your home. Many people cross your path. Of the visitors who have sat at your dinner table, not all have tales of danger, but they all have experiences you can learn from. You can see the world through their eyes and words. Our kids' favorites were the ones who were on fire for the Lord, who connected with them at their age level, and who had a good sense of humor.

Perhaps you travel with your parents more than your peers in conjunction with your dad's preaching itinerary, so you get to meet more people and have more fascinating cross-cultural experiences. Our children, for example, have visited Israel and Europe—including the beautiful Swiss Alps—as well as many of the American states. Meeting many of God's people and witnessing God's beauty in the realm of nature are life-enriching experiences.

God's people come in a fascinating variety; it is always interesting to study them to see what makes them tick. Apply what you learn to your future life. Our kids have had thoughts like these: "I think it's wise how he manages his finances according to biblical principles." "I like her style of dressing—cool yet modest." "Hmm, I'm never going to chew with my mouth open like him." "I like how he communicates with perceptive questions and a kind, steady gaze." "He really cares about sinners and wants them to know God; I want that same zeal."

You never know who will walk through the doors of your church. Be ready to welcome them. Move out of your comfort zone by tuning in to others' discomfort and making them comfortable. Learn empathy. See the positive in people. Like—yes, love—people. Be helpful. Develop people skills in a way that fits your personality. Soak up experiences—yours and others'—and learn from them. Learn how to ask good questions. Take advantage of these valuable opportunities. Love what is good and do good to others.

The Burdens

Let's be honest. When you read the title of this chapter, some of you thought, "I am not enjoying being a PK, and I don't see many blessings or benefits—just burdens." We wish we could speak with you face-to-face, but we can't. So we would like to offer some perspectives on dealing with your situation.

The most important question to ask, whether you are a PK or not, is, "Am I right with God?" If you are not, nothing else matters. You need to make peace with God; otherwise, you are not ready to meet Him, and you are rebelling against Him. Rebellion is bad news; it guarantees those who embrace it a troubled life.

But there is bright hope! Be honest with God; tell Him everything on your heart—even the bad stuff. He knows it anyway. Beg Him to change your heart, because you can't (or won't) do it yourself. Seek counsel from someone godly and trustworthy. Pray and read and search until He does His powerful work in you, until the Holy Spirit lives in you, and you know that Jesus's blood paid for your sins. Repent and believe on Him!

Once this matter is resolved, your foundation is sure. We can go on from here! But what if you have been a believer for a while, and you are still grappling with the challenges of being a PK? If Jesus Christ is the Rock of your life, we can find common ground. There are solutions in His Word. Let's find them.

Your expectations determine your attitude (Prov. 15:15). If you expect life to be smooth and easy, you will be disappointed. So let's take a look at your expectations. Here are some truths that you need to face, along with some coping mechanisms. We call it *reality therapy*.

Others' expectations can put stressful demands on you. No, it's not fair that church members expect you to behave better than other kids or to know Scripture better. It's not fair that they think the pastor's son should grow up to be a minister. It's not fair that you are singled out from your peers because you are a PK.

The problem with going down the "it's-not-fair road" is that it leads to a dead end for this simple reason: neither you nor we can change people's expectations. We can tell you, however, the happy news that you are not answerable to these people. Just look beyond people to God. You are answerable to God and to your parents. So try to think in terms of that. Share your frustrations with your parents or a trusted friend. Pray—and then pray some more. Then just leave unreasonable expectations be. You are a regular kid. Your family is a regular family. Life is primarily about God and you and your family anyway.

You get frustrated because your dad is on duty 24/7. He gets called away when you are doing something fun together. He is sometimes in another zone because he is preoccupied with church troubles. It's hard to be uprooted when your dad takes a call to another church. You don't have a lot of money because the church is small and not rich.

We understand, but please remember that nearly every family has to make sacrifices of some sort for their dad's occupation. Some dads work the evening shift and see their kids only on weekends. Many families struggle financially. Some dads don't care about the souls of their kids. Some dads swear, beat up their kids, or take no responsibility at all. Some dads—in fact, many dads—don't function at all in their kids' lives.

Some dads drink their lives away. Last week we went to a wedding, and the dad wasn't available to walk his daughter down the aisle. It was painful for the bride and her sister, who was matron of honor. The bride had told her dad, who lives out of state, that she would like him to walk her down the aisle, but only if he sobered up, because she didn't want him making a messy scene at the wedding or reception. And the dad wanted to do it, but he was enslaved to his bottle, so he wasn't able to be present for his daughter's wedding.

We are asking you to try to understand. We are asking you to see the positive and to count your blessings. We hope if your dad gets called away to an unexpected pastoral visit that he makes up for it later—the big picture is that he spends quality and sufficient quantity time with you. Your dad bears the burdens of his flock, and he is called to work diligently for the cause of Christ. If you feel like you lack your dad's attention, don't act out or rebel. Talk with him respectfully and ask him, "Dad, you are good to me in many ways, but sometimes I feel like you are more dedicated to the church than you are to me. I really need you to hang out with me more. Don't misunderstand, Dad, I really do love you—that's why I want to be with you more."

One more thought on this: though much has been spoken and written about pastors being too busy for their children, don't forget that your dad has often been able to break away at surprising times. Sure, he is not at home as much as most dads on Saturday, with the Lord's Day near and his sermons often not yet finished, but what other dad can break away when you need him for something after you come home for school? There is flexibility in your dad's schedule that can at least make up for some of the long hours that he must put in to be an effective minister of the gospel.

Your home is like Central Station—people coming and going, with or without appointments. You have little privacy. You feel like you have to share everything. You have a couple of choices here. Embrace it and enjoy it! Or see if you can talk to your parents in a reasonable way and work out a mix of being involved and sometimes being on your own. We think they will understand. We tried to reach a balance with our kids. When we sensed that they were getting tired of company, we backed off and had family time or gave them more private time. But we would encourage you to push yourself beyond your comfort zone. At first you might not feel very social, but you might be surprised at how much you enjoy visitors and benefit from them when you stretch yourself a bit.

You see hypocrisy in the church, and you see the human flaws in your dad, too. We do not excuse hypocrisy in the least. Remember that Jesus didn't come to this earth to save the righteous, but sinners. The church is compared to an emergency room—just a bunch of broken people. Have an honest, heartfelt talk with your parents about your concerns. Don't expect perfection from them or any human being. You will have disappointments. Satan loves to mix it up in the church. The church is a flock of sinful, wandering sheep striving to stay on the straight and narrow, with God's help, by running the race set before them and looking to Jesus (Heb. 12:1–2). That includes you and us. Give people grace. Know human nature. Know yourself. Seek God's grace for them and for yourself. Love them. Most of all, love Christ who died for us. He says, "Learn of me; for I am meek and lowly" (Matt. 11:29 KJV).

We cannot condone rebellious behavior—or even rebellion that is just brewing in your heart. But we can urge you to get to the bottom of what is driving you. Your parents love you, even if they don't respond perfectly. Be honest with yourself and with them and with God. Share your heart with your parents. Be respectful to them.

And do remember: your behavior is your responsibility. Own it! Think about where it will lead you. Don't blame others for issues that are your own. Only God can help with that. Pray for strength to divert your course to a godly direction. In every family there is give and take—sacrifices need to be made by all. But hopefully balance is in the big picture. Pray for yourself, your parents, and others.

Then embrace your life, and you will enjoy it and be content. It is exciting to walk in God's will. A joyful life doesn't necessarily mean an easy life. What seems like a burden now can be seen as a blessing later, as many PKs have testified. Pray through the good times and the bad. Ann Benton, a PK mom, advises, "Don't let what you don't have rob you of what you have." Count your blessings; name them one by one.

Conclusion

Finally, we've often experienced that the happiest people in life are those who are staying closest to the Word of God on a daily basis. Are you reading and searching the Bible every day? That can make a huge difference. You can't have a really good relationship with people if you have a mediocre or poor relationship with God. All relationships are a two-way street—they involve two-way communication. God speaks to us in His Word; we speak back to Him in prayer. Both are essential—and usually, when we keep up with both, life's burdens can be embraced as blessings, for then we learn to trust God and thank Him even for the hard times. Then, though others may see you as a PK, you will see yourself primarily as a CK—Christ's kid. And when that becomes real for you, you will begin to learn to thank Christ and your Father in every situation, because you will see that all things happen according to His will, for His glory, and for your good (Rom. 8:28). Once your eyes are open to that, you will also become a TK—a thankful kid. First Thessalonians 5:18 puts it so well: "In every thing give thanks: for this is the will of God in Christ Jesus concerning you" (KJV).

Your brother and sister in Christ,

Joel and Mary

Joel R. Beeke is president and professor of systematic theology and homiletics at Puritan Reformed Theological Seminary. He has been married to his wife, **Mary Beeke**, since 1989. They are blessed with three children and seven grandchildren and serve as a pastor and pastor's wife of the Heritage Reformed Congregation in Grand Rapids, Michigan, since 1986.

FRIENDSHIPS
The Glorious Gift of Extended Family

Terry and Emily Johnson

Mom and Dad formed a dynamic team as parents: they created a haven for their children that I hope to emulate one day. They certainly enforced rules (like no cell phones until you turn sixteen, no TV on Sundays, etc.), but they always explained *why* they did *what* they did. And besides the no-cell-phone-after-ten-p.m. rule, I never felt the need to question their rationale. Our home became a refuge in which I fled social angst, explored cultural questions, and sang the soundtrack of *The Sound of Music* without feeling sixty years old. Mom always kept us laughing, while Dad—well, he laughed with her, too. Oftentimes, I think people marvel to learn that ministers have actual personalities when they leave their pulpits. Nearly every time I tell a story and happen to mention my dad during that story, the whole crowd roars. At the end of the story, someone will comment, "Wait, your *dad* was watching the Dodgers game, too? *Seriously*?" (cue laughter)…as though my dad comes home and continues preaching to us in his long black robe.

I can testify that Dad (both now and twenty-three years ago) sings his old fraternity songs, grills chicken wings quite well, hits the volleyball with me in the backyard, and spends Saturdays in the fall watching college football.

Growing up in the Johnson home combined the best of Chick fil-A and T. J. Maxx: it provided a comforting consistency and order to our lives, though one seldom saw the same thing twice. For example, you'd better believe we had devotions every morning, but whether or not Dad would make us sing five psalms or six was always a toss-up (#psalmsingingjokes). Similarly, we hosted people from all ages and backgrounds nearly every Sunday, yet Mom never changed her brunch menu (anyone who has enjoyed her brunch knows why). In all seriousness, Mom and Dad instilled in us a desire and ability to interact, socialize, and appreciate many different types of people. Our church, like most, consists of people who represent a wide range of age groups, personalities, and opinions. Rather than allow us to seek out people like ourselves, Mom and Dad always put us in situations where we didn't really have a choice *except* to interact with church members. Furthermore, none of our blood relatives lived in Savannah, so this sense of church family seemed heightened in our home. Some (maybe even most) of my fondest childhood memories revolve around older church members investing in me and teaching me how to live generously and selflessly. One member regularly took me and my little brother to Chuck E. Cheese. Another member always gave us free dental care and even his old cars. One lady purchased homecoming and prom dresses for my sister and me each year!

I think that, oftentimes, we feel a strange mix of emotions as pastors' kids: humbled, supported, exhausted, embittered, watched. One moment we feel incredibly blessed by the unprompted generosity of a church member. Yet the next moment, spiteful members silence us as they seem eager to witness any misstep. Thankfully, my parents worked to combat these burdens and constantly reminded us that people have complex, unknown stories. They urged us to give grace to others, even when we didn't feel it reciprocated. And I can safely say that without my parents having reinforced the importance of community within the church body, I seriously doubt I would value and cherish those types of multigenerational friendships as I do now.

Your fellow PK,

Abby

Dear Pastor's Kid,

Recently at a dinner party given by new members of the church, our oldest child, now out of the house and married, was asked, "So what was it like growing up in the minister's family?" His answer: "Aside from certain fishbowl aspects, I think all of us would say the positive outweighed the negative." When he told me (Emily) later about it, I surmised that his four younger siblings would wholeheartedly agree with that synopsis. After spending nearly thirty-one years in Savannah with the same congregation, we consider our church extended family. As with one's blood-built family, there are no perfect relationships. We encounter the equivalents of meddling aunts, the snide and snarky teens, and the blunt and bombastic fathers-in-law. There are plenty of well-intentioned dragons, yet as with one's family, we continue to live with imperfect patience, knowing that God is working on their sanctification just as He is our own. Remember, try not to drown in the fishbowl.

Hindsight is twenty-twenty. Oh, to be able to do some things over again—especially with regard to our children and their relationships within the church body. We were so incredibly busy having five babies in seven years and then subsequently raising them that many times we lost sight of what was truly important and lasting. Our advice and counsel to you would be to extend lots of grace and patience to your parents. It matters not whether you are an only child or one of eight, whether your father is pastor of a large congregation or a small one. He is in charge of souls. And those souls can be complicated, demanding, prickly, and profoundly sad. This takes a toll on the preacher's family. If it does not, perhaps something is amiss.

Our children were front-row observers to the heights and depths of church life. Preaching the gospel week after week to sinners, no matter how sanctified they are, can be fraught with conflict. "Is So-and-So mad at Dad?" was a question asked with regularity. This, I think, is peculiar to the pastor's home. In an effort to protect the children from bitterness and the messiness of ministry, I (Emily) kept them (and sometimes myself, regretfully) from forming more friendships within the church. Instead of praying Psalm 35:1, "Plead my cause, O LORD, with those who strive with me," I put up defenses and hunkered down maybe more than I should have. I built a wall around our family, over which few could climb. But what if we had invited contentious folks over for pancakes? What if we had asked them over for coffee and dessert? What if I had "done ministry" in spite of the fear of potential awkwardness? These are thoughts that my older (and wiser) heart ponders often. "But," as Martyn Lloyd Jones wrote in *Spiritual Depression*, "let us go further and realize that to dwell on the past simply causes failure in the present." The Lord is gracious to those who seek Him. While I regret that I did not seek Him more when things got dicey in the manse, "love will cover a multitude of sins" (1 Peter 4:8). His love for us extends above all of our poor decisions and sinful reactions. Thanks be to God.

Background

We were barely six months married when we arrived in Savannah. We had each other but knew no one else. This is often the case for ministers. Most are called away from family. Many are called far away. Clergy families sacrifice the regular help, the support, the encouragement (and also the interference, annoyance, etc.) of immediate family. From 1988 to 1995, we had five children in quick succession. We had no family nearby to help with child-rearing or schooling. Yet, the church is family: We are the household of God (Eph. 2:19). Church members and, more broadly, all believers are our brothers and sisters. God is our Father and Christ is our elder Brother. Jesus promised that those who leave their homes and families will receive far more homes and brothers and sisters and mothers and fathers *in this life* and the life to come (Mark 10:30). Have we found this to be true? Indeed we have, and so will you. God has supplied all our needs according to His riches in glory in Christ Jesus, including the need for family (Phil. 4:19). Several poignant examples come to mind.

Our Marine Leaves

Our son Sam left for Marine Base Quantico outside of Washington, DC, on January 5, 2014. He was to report to OCS (Officer Candidate School) there the following afternoon. Our family had never been through a separation like this before. Ever. Aside from taking our kids to college, we had never experienced such a painful departure. Yet even more troubling than this separation was the trauma that awaited Sam: his drill instructors dictated his every move. They enforced harsh, meticulous, rigid rules: no communication with the outside world (with the exception of letters), no food in care packages (not even gum), no talking in first person (he was forced to refer to himself as "Candidate"). For the first few weeks, we had no way to contact him, or vice versa. How could we possibly endure this for twelve more weeks? After our first phone call from Sam, we were bereft. He was never going to be able to do this. He was out in one of the coldest winters on recent record, breaking the Quigley ice with his rifle so he could crawl under barbed wire through the freezing water. Meanwhile, the drill instructors were barking in ears and faces, terrorizing breakfast, lunch, and dinner.

A little angel was sent to me the next morning in the form of Chief Warrant Officer Three Michael Spencer. Michael was a deacon at our church, the father of four, and a veteran military pilot. He had been deployed numerous times. He stood with me in the church lane for thirty minutes calming me down, encouraging me, and assuring me that "they had Sam right where they wanted him." I cannot tell you the balm that Michael was for us that day and for many days to come as Sam's training continued throughout 2014.

Our good man Sam also got the "award" for *the most mail at OCS*. He was called up for mail so often that people grew suspicious. "I have a really large support system" was his response to the jealous looks and comments. What do you think *all that* support was doing for *that PK* right about then? The cards and letters kept him afloat in the face of incredible adversity and against all kinds of odds. While we have a very tight nuclear family, I'm not sure exactly how that year would have panned out without our church family. In fact, I don't even want to think about it. God used the family He had given Sam, both blood-built and covenant, to push him through, up until that point, the toughest year of his life.

Home from Kuwait

We needed a way to say thank you. The older folks in our church had prayed for Sam not only through 2014 at Quantico but also through a deployment to the Middle East from 2015 to 2016. So many people "do" for the minister's family that we frequently find ourselves wondering,

How on earth do we ever give back? One tangible way, we have realized over time, is the giving of yourself, your time and attention. We checked with Sam to make sure it was fine with him, and he immediately and wholeheartedly agreed. So, when Sam returned for post-deployment leave, we had a "Breakfast with Sam" for all the older saints. Some remember the day he was born. Others were newer to the church but had taken a keen interest in his military experience. Almost every man present had been involved in praying for Sam every Tuesday morning at our men's prayer breakfast at the church.

As the second born (and only fifteen months behind oldest brother, Drew), Sam was never the verbal or social Johnson. Not great with small talk, he would let Drew or his sisters talk. But not this morning! Sam was the host and the star of the show. The folks were so grateful to be invited, and Sam was so grateful to thank them personally for their prayers. As Sam greeted each guest at the door, my eyes overflowed with tears at the sweetness of our extended family's love for us. He also, much to the older folks' delight, played hymns on our beloved piano. It was quite a scene; as we walked the elderly folks to their cars, Sam banged out "Guide Me, O Thou Great Jehovah" for all of earth to hear. It was a perfect picture of the older generation ministering to the younger and then that generation, in turn, blessing the older saints. Those are the sorts of things that happen in the church and nowhere else, if you can keep your eyes open to see them.

Church Wedding

Having a daughter marrying out of the minister's home is a challenge for anyone—even professional event planners and "Miss Manners." Ours was doubly unusual in that Sally had been born into this congregation, went to college in the state, and then came back and worked in our hometown after graduation. How would we *ever* come up with a guest list? Well, lots of tears, arguments, and angry emails later, the obvious hit us like a ton of bricks. Everyone's invited, of course. How could it be any other way? How does one divide up one's family? Who would do that? Certainly not us. Why did we not figure this out right away? Why did it take so long? We were looking at it all wrong. We were being stingy, counting heads and mouths, trying to parse friendships and acquaintances.

One night after the evening service, one of the older ladies in the church came up to Terry and said, "I am so excited about Sally's wedding. I remember when she was just a little girl." This lady would not have even made the guest list cutoff. That's when we asked, "What are we doing?" From then on, though we had our bumps along the way, the wedding was celebrated and talked about freely by any and all. Lori Irish, who runs a program for those transitioning from jail life to life on the "outside," was one of our most enthusiastic guests. She was so pleased to be included, and, honestly, it would not have been the same without her and our whole "family" celebrating with us. Initially our daughter's new in-law family intimidated me. Both sides of her groom's family are large and travel for all family weddings. When we changed our perspective concerning the guest list, we realized that we in fact had the larger family, far larger.

The night of the wedding, the congregation, our extended family, gave us the best gift ever. The singing almost lifted our beautiful domed ceiling right off its foundation. We were transported to another world as our entire congregation sang "And Can It Be" at the top of their lungs and to the honor and praise of our great God.

Home Improvement Contractor

PKs are pretty much always looking for and needing jobs—paying ones. The boys were forever jealous that the girls got to babysit—"$50 for watching TV all night." Ugh. One summer our youngest child needed to make more money than he could being a camp counselor. He asked a man in our church for a summer job. When he told us about it, we were very surprised and inwardly thought, "Oh, dear Ben. We're not sure this is what you really want to do for the summer." This man had worked on our house many times before. He didn't accept laziness. He could sniff out character flaws quicker than a skinny minute. He was also not shy about spiritual things and conversations. He pulled no punches about hours, time sheets, quality of the work, and integrity. He didn't even believe in taking a break to eat lunch! A meal in the middle of the day made you sleepy and slowed you down. He preferred an orange and a granola bar. Ben, on the other hand, was used to consuming two thousand calories at lunch alone. Who, or what in the world, was our nineteen-year-old college boy doing working eight to ten hours a day with *this guy*? It was true to say, we were nervous.

Well, of course, as ever, God had other plans—for Ben, Dave, and all of us. As the long, tedious hours of painting, sanding, and sheet-rocking wore on, a warm friendship formed. Soon Ben was quoting "Diesel Dave" at the dinner table. We noticed that Ben was becoming more thoughtful about things. He was thinking through situations and problem solving with new maturity. There was even a situation that involved a choice between watching a favorite team in the March Madness Basketball Tournament or going to a Maundy (Last Supper) Thursday service at church. Ben was in college, and we now allowed him to make decisions like these for himself. He fussed and fumed about it. He gave me (Emily) every argument in the book as to why he should/could/would stay home to watch the game. I (surprising even myself) said very little. I will never forget Ben racing down the stairs and out the door with me for the Maundy Thursday service. I was pleasantly surprised and wondered about the change in plans. It was then that it hit me. Diesel Dave had become not only a boss, but a friend, mentor, and encourager in the faith. Later David would tell us about the talk they had had that week about the whole situation. This would never have happened had the friendship not been forged over countless hours working together and lunches of clementines and Cliff bars. David took Ben and poured into him and, as a result, had made a little disciple. We were reminded again of the wonderful "extended family" within the church.

Church Family

What we lost in babysitters was more than compensated in church family. Educating five children in Christian and prep schools is expensive. College is worse. Two church families saw it as their mission to help us pay all the tuition bills, the scope of which we are embarrassed even to mention. Vacationing with five children can also be expensive. Twice a generous family took us with them (all seven of us) on luxury vacations to distant realms, refusing to allow us to spend a dime. Another treated us to a Disneyworld extravaganza. Church members came to our children's recitals and athletic events, encouraging them in failure and cheering them on to success. One gracious retired couple took us in for six weeks while our home was being renovated. The children all have this man's phone number in their cell phones, as he has been for our family the "car expert," advising us about repairs, purchases, and roadside emergencies. Several members became grandparental stand-ins, known as "Mamma Mearl" and "Mama Marion" and "Big Daddy." College students and interns served as uncles and big brothers. Sally even had her own "Mary Fairy Godmother" who would appear to sprinkle her life with outings and treats.

The church is neither male nor female, Jew nor Greek, slave nor free (Gal. 3:28). So also it is neither young nor old. We find throughout the epistles exhortations being addressed to marrieds and singles (1 Corinthians 7), young and old (Titus 2), parents and children (Ephesians 6), rich and poor (1 Timothy 6), and Jews and Greeks (Acts 10–11). The obvious but often overlooked implication is that these diverse groups were sitting in the same church when a given epistle was read. There weren't churches for old people or young people. Generational segregation was not practiced.

Our church has sought to mimic the rich diversity of the New Testament church. We have not allowed our public services to favor the cultural preferences of one group over another, whether ethnic or generational. As a result, we have enjoyed a healthy balance of young and old; white collar and blue collar; rich, poor, and middle class. Because our services, especially regarding music and format, don't belong to a group, they belong to everyone. What this has meant for our children is significant.

When our oldest son returned home after a semester at Wheaton College, we first noticed a particular benefit of a generationally diverse church. Before and after the service a steady stream of our members, young dads and moms and, especially important, older men and women, approached him and asked how he was surviving at college a thousand miles from home. Interesting, we thought. Our children leave the nest known by dozens of nonfamily members who will interrogate them when they return. Of course the questioners do so kindly and with genuine interest. Still, what this represents is *healthy accountability*. They leave home not as autonomous individuals, but as part of a church family. This is an important part of the identity that they carry with them. They know that their behavior impacts not only their natural family but also the church family. They go with an extra layer of motivation, both restraining destructive impulses and motivating good conduct. We are grateful to have this accountability boost provided by our church family, and so should you be glad.

Family Feuds

Finally, all has not been roses. Ironically, the worst things that have happened to our children have come not from members but from other ministers, who, in conjunction with their children, have hurled false accusations at them, the falseness of which took considerable pain-filled time finally to establish. Setting that aside, we lament that too many members have *not* regarded the church as family. We have spent years pouring our lives into the lives of others, only to have them leave. On several occasions they have left without a word. They just walked away. They never looked back. They never even said goodbye. These can be disillusioning experiences.

Not infrequently our most troublesome church members have been those with whom we have spent the most time, made the most effort, and expended more of the church resources, financial and otherwise. This perhaps is the most befuddling of all aspects of the ministry. Membership vows are meant to tie members together in a covenant family. Too many members have treated those vows with contempt and broken our hearts in the process. Don't be surprised by the bad behavior of church members, and don't be discouraged. Churches are made up of sinners—redeemed sinners, but sinners nonetheless.

Thankfully, many others have honored the church's covenant in spite of conflicts. Sometimes reconciliation takes years. Often one must stay put to see positive outcomes. Long-term ministries provide time for differences to be reconciled. This leads to our last story.

Twenty-one years ago we had a painful argument with a deeply committed family in the church. We were both surprised and disappointed by the other family's point of view. Actually, our surprise was disbelief. How could they see things as they did? The separation was real and palpable and even awkward. Communication all but shut down for a considerable time. One Sunday in the midst of this crisis, I (Emily) walked by the nursery, peering in the window only to see the mother of this alienated family rocking my infant son, tears streaming down her face. I walked in and hugged her. No words were exchanged. Nothing needed to be said. We had an understanding. They weren't going anywhere, and neither were we. Over time, the wounds healed. Our daughters became and remain each other's soul mates. Their father became the clerk of session and perhaps my husband's most zealous supporter. Finally, and quite providentially, our oldest son married their youngest daughter, the same one who was our daughter's very best friend. Our joy overflowed at the wedding as the congregation celebrated this most happy of occasions.

PKs pay a price. There is no question about it. The fishbowl is uncomfortable, the expectations of others irritating. Yet we think that the benefits far outweigh the costs. Yes, you have to deal with the frustration of the church's imperfect family members. Yes, you have to guard your heart from self-indulgent cynicism and bitterness. Still, God's people are a blessing. The kingdom of God is a refuge. The church is a family. God's children, even His clergy children, are especially treasured.

And so, our concluding thoughts to you are these:

- Don't hunker down and build that wall that folks can't scale.

- Do be willing to enter into friendship with those of every size, shape, stripe, and background.

- Be gracious in receiving those gifts that church members might give.

- Never give up on a friendship in the church. It might take a long time to heal. Be ready and willing for the healing to take place.

- And finally, do not burn any bridges! If you or your family have been hurt by others, perhaps even had your good name slandered, do not destroy the bridge by which the Lord may make all things new again. You'll be surprised by who walks over that bridge.

We have loved sharing our experiences with you. May the Lord encourage you in your friendships within His local body.

Warmly in Christ,

Terry and Emily Johnson

Terry and Emily Johnson live in Savannah, Georgia. Terry is the senior minister at the Independent Presbyterian church there. They are the parents of five, parents-in-law to four, and (currently) grandparents to four. IPC has been nurturing the Johnsons since 1987.

LOVING THE CHURCH
Pressing On Through Family Highs and Lows

Tom and Donna Ascol

When first asked to contribute a chapter for this book, Tom and Donna Ascol turned to the experts, their six children. Numerous discussions over years of family dinners, hours of searching God's Word to understand the role of the church in the life of a Christian, and thousands of prayers lifted for the hearts of children growing up in the ministry spotlight have culminated in what you are about to read. Through thirty-plus years of full-time pastoral ministry, our parents have faithfully loved their PKs, shepherding our hearts, guiding our steps, pointing us to Christ, and challenging us to learn to love the church the way Jesus loves her. We have watched them fight for this love when ministry is hard and seen them celebrate over the work of God among His people. We can think of no other couple more qualified to speak to pastors' kids about this topic.

In addition to being our amazing parents, Tom and Donna have served more than thirty years at Grace Baptist Church in Southwest Florida, where Tom is a pastor and Donna a longtime teacher of teenage girls' Sunday school classes. While we know they love being Mom and Dad, we enjoy seeing them embrace the roles of Noni and Paps to their nine grandchildren.

We love them beyond what we can express and thank God for the privilege of growing up in their home. Our prayer for you is that this chapter will help you love the church more.

Warmly in Christ,
The Ascol PKs: Sarah Ascol, Rebecca Sissons, Rachel Davis, Joel Ascol, Grace Regnier, and Hannah Ascol

Dear Pastor's Kid,

Growing up in a pastor's home brings with it many blessings. I'm sure you treasure the opportunities you have had to meet wonderful Christian servants from around the world who have not only ministered in your church but also have enjoyed hospitality in your home. Hasn't it also been at least a tiny bit fun sometimes to know what Dad is going to say in his sermon before others in the congregation? More importantly, hasn't the Lord blessed you to let you have your pastor so readily accessible to you?

But we know that with those blessings come some real challenges. No doubt you have seen family plans change at the last minute because of an unexpected need in the church that has demanded your dad's attention. Then there are all those expectations that subtly—and often not-so-subtly—are placed on you because, after all, "you are the pastor's kid." We know that gets old and can tempt you to put up walls of protection that keep you from getting too close to church people. Those walls can become higher and thicker when church members act hurtfully and sinfully toward you or your family.

One of the greatest challenges our children have faced is to receive God's Word preached week-by-week by their very flawed dad. Even the best of fathers have weaknesses and blemishes. Tragically, intimate awareness of those blemishes has led some pastors' children to grow indifferent or even opposed to Christ's church and the message it proclaims.

We have seen that happen far too often, and we certainly understand it. We also grieve over it. Why? Because we know that opposition, resentment, or even indifference toward the church will spiritually destroy a person. We do not want to see that happen to you. So, as we have prayed for you, we thought it might be helpful to offer you a few thoughts about the importance of learning to love the church as a pastor's kid.

There are so many blessings and challenges that go with growing up in a pastor's home that it is easy to forget that the same responsibilities that belong to every Christian also belong to Christian children of pastors. One of the most important things you can do is to remind yourself regularly that if you are born again, you are, first and foremost, a child of God. You are a follower of Jesus Christ. He is your Lord. His commandments are not only right, they are also good. The responsibilities that He places on believers are for our greatest benefit.

This includes the responsibility He has given us to love the church. In fact, it simply is not possible to love Christ as we ought without loving the church.

Christ Loves the Church

Stop and think about it. The call to be a Christian is a call to trust Christ, to follow Him, and to be conformed to Him. Romans 8:29 indicates that this is at the heart of God's purpose in saving us: "Whom He foreknew, He also predestined to be conformed to the image of His Son, that He might be the firstborn among many brethren." What that means is that God intends for us to become more like Jesus in our character and behavior. In 2 Corinthians 3:18 Paul says that this goal will be reached through a process of "being transformed into" the image of Christ.

If God's goal for us is to become like Christ, and if we are to be progressively changed into His image, then we need to think deeply about what Jesus is actually like. One thing that the New Testament makes clear is that Jesus loves the church. Paul says, "Christ also loved the church and gave Himself for her" (Eph. 5:25). This means that Jesus loved the whole church (sometimes it is called the universal church) in such a way that He gave His life for her by laying it down for her on the cross.

If you really love Jesus, then shouldn't you love what He loves? He loves the church, and so should His followers. We encourage you to embrace this as both your calling and goal.

Part of what it means to grow in Christlikeness includes growing in your love for His church. That means more than merely loving the idea of the church or even loving the universal church (all of God's people who have ever lived or will live). It means loving YOUR church—the one to which you belong right now.

Jesus Loves Your Church and So Must You

That can be hard, we know. Often it is easier to love the church "in theory" than to love a particular church. A friend shared this little poem that, though humorous, is often all too true:

To dwell above with saints we love, oh that will be glory.
But to dwell below with saints we know, that's another story!

Paul Loved the Church

How can you learn to love those saints below with whom you rub
elbows day in and day out? The saints who sometimes ignore you, hurt
you, and disappoint you? What does loving your church look like when
you have seen church members mistreat your dad or harshly criticize
your mom? How can you not only avoid bitterness but also show true
love for church members who have excluded you or embarrassed you
because of who your dad is?

The apostle Paul provides us with real help at this point in the way
that we see him loving particular churches, even when they had hurt and
disappointed him. Perhaps the greatest example of this is his love for the
church at Corinth. Paul spent over a year of his life planting that church.
He wrote his greatest description of love in order to encourage the Corinthian Christians to grow spiritually by loving each other sincerely.

You are familiar with that description in 1 Corinthians 13, where he
writes that "love suffers long and is kind; love does not envy; love does
not parade itself, is not puffed up; does not behave rudely, does not seek
its own, is not provoked, thinks no evil; does not rejoice in iniquity,
but rejoices in the truth; bears all things, believes all things, hopes all
things, endures all things. Love never fails" (vv. 4–8).

Jerry Bridges has restated this in a way that makes it easier to use in
your personal relationships.

I am patient with you because I love you and want to forgive you.

I am kind to you because I love you and want to help you.

I do not envy your possessions or your gifts because I love you and
want you to have the best.

I do not boast about my attainments because I love you and want
to hear about yours.

I am not proud because I love you and want to esteem you
before myself.

I am not rude because I love you and care about your feelings.

I am not self-seeking because I love you and want to meet your needs.

I am not easily angered by you because I love you and want to overlook your offenses.

I do not keep a record of your wrongs because I love you, and "love covers a multitude of sins."

You can quickly see how this applies to the way that we should think about and treat our church if we truly love it. True love is not just a feeling. It is action. Just before He was arrested, Jesus emphasized this point to His apostles. He said, "A new commandment I give to you, that you love one another; as I have loved you, that you also love one another" (John 13:34). Later, John reminds us that we must not merely "love in word or in tongue, but in deed and in truth" (1 John 3:18). In other words, as followers of Jesus who have experienced His love in His sacrificial death for our sins, we must love one another; that is, we must love the church in the same way that we have been loved.

How can we learn to do that? How can we learn to love the church this way, especially at those times when sin in the church is so obvious and painful?

Grace Empowers Love

We are empowered to love by the grace of God that we receive in Jesus Christ. To know that you are a sinner against God and that you justly deserve His everlasting wrath is the foundation to appreciating the depth of God's grace in salvation.

In 1 Timothy 1:13–15 Paul describes himself this way: "I was formerly a blasphemer, a persecutor, and an insolent man…. I obtained mercy because I did it ignorantly in unbelief. And the grace of our Lord was exceedingly abundant, with faith and love which are in Christ Jesus. This is a faithful saying and worthy of all acceptance, that Christ Jesus came into the world to save sinners, of whom I am chief."

Paul's honest look at the wickedness of his sin caused him to value God's grace all the more. Paul never got over the fact that God gave up His only begotten Son in order to save him from his sin. Though he deserved condemnation, he received forgiveness, all because of the grace of God. That grace, he says, overflowed to him with love in Christ Jesus.

In other words, because he had received grace, he could not help but extend grace and respond in love.

We can see this in how Paul loved the church at Corinth. Even a quick read through 1 Corinthians reveals that the church there had many serious problems. There were people in the church who had turned on Paul and were stirring up a great deal of trouble. They were immature, selfish, arrogant, sexually immoral, abusing the Lord's Table, sinfully divorcing, arguing over spiritual gifts, disrupting worship services, and denying the resurrection of Jesus.

That church was a mess! It would have been easy to walk away from it, to become frustrated with it or to write it off completely. Paul, however, demonstrated real love for it. In fact, he began his first letter to the church by telling them: "I thank my God always concerning you for the grace of God which was given to you by Christ Jesus" (1 Cor. 1:4).

How could Paul say that? He could say these things because he understood the nature of salvation by grace—that the only kinds of people God saves are real sinners. Jesus said, "I have not come to call the righteous, but sinners, to repentance" (Luke 5:32). If you know that you are a sinner before God, that is great news, isn't it?

Paul knew that sin remains even within the best of Christians and that new believers especially can be easily led astray. That is how he could speak so warmly to them even when he knew he must go on to rebuke them sharply for the sin and foolishness into which they had fallen.

Paul made the effort to commend God's grace at work among them, not because he was wearing rose-colored glasses and, for the moment, had forgotten about all their problems. Rather, he celebrated the grace of God in the Corinthians because he not only understood the doctrine of grace but understood the life of grace. He himself had been saved by grace, and he knew that the only reason anyone ever moves forward in the Christian life is by God's grace. As he puts it in 1 Corinthians 15:10, "By the grace of God I am what I am."

Paul realized that, though these Corinthian church members had lots of flaws, they were nevertheless children of God, which meant that they were objects of His grace. Despite their weaknesses and flaws, God was at work in them. God had given them the gospel, united them to Christ, and would hold them fast until the return of Christ.

It was with this conviction of who they were and what God was doing among them that Paul wrote to them. He didn't let their problems keep him from remembering that they were part of God's family. As such, he knew that God was at work in them. So, Paul started his letter by calling attention to that work and celebrating God's grace in them.

This is one of the most helpful disciplines to develop if you want to grow in your love for your church. Stop and think about the ways that God is at work in your own life and in the lives of your brothers and sisters in your congregation. When you talk to fellow church members who have unjustly questioned your dad's motives in a congregational meeting, consciously try to remember that you are talking to people in whom God is working by His grace. Look for evidences of that grace. Has their language or schedule changed out of devotion to the Lord? Do they serve others in any way? Are they attentive to the Word? Have they expressed repentance over sin? Do they pray? Are they pressing on in the faith despite setbacks and trials they have faced?

These and other observable traits may not seem very dramatic, but they can be signs of God's grace at work in His people. As we learn to look for them, point them out, and even celebrate them, we will be empowered to love the people in whom we see them. This kind of alertness to evidences of grace will inevitably stir us to love the church. So work to develop a deep appreciation for God's grace in your own life and in the lives of your fellow church members.

Forgiveness

Of course, if you are involved in the life of a church for very long, you can count on being sinned against by fellow believers. Someone will say something hurtful or overlook you or misrepresent you in ways that leave you wounded and discouraged simply because your dad is the pastor.

When you are sinned against in an obvious and deliberate way, then you must resolve the issue the way that Jesus instructs in Matthew 18:15–18. Go to the one who sinned against you and work it out privately. (This can be especially hard if that person is someone older than you or someone who is in leadership in the church. If that is the case, engage the counsel and help of someone you trust in the church.)

Hopefully, if real sin is involved, repentance and forgiveness will happen, and reconciliation will occur. If matters are not resolved by that effort, then continue to seek their repentance and offer forgiveness and reconciliation by following Jesus's further instructions for the sake of all parties involved and for the well-being of the whole church.

Very often, however, you will be offended not by blatant sin but by thoughtlessness or carelessness. Perhaps you don't get invited to an activity because your friends did not think "the PK" would fit in. You are not asked to serve in a capacity that you really desire. You are silenced in class because you already "know all the answers." Your preferences are not taken into consideration when certain plans are made. In other words, you are expected to behave, think, and respond in certain ways simply because you are your father's child and then judged as failing when you don't appear to measure up. It is easy to be hurt in dozens of ways like these.

So, how should you respond when these things happen? It is easy to pretend not to care and to let the hurt fester until it hardens you against the church. Or you can strike out in revenge in order to "teach a lesson" or to show others how it feels. Some people see being offended as a legitimate reason to leave a church. The Bible, however, never regards being offended as appropriate grounds for a Christian to respond in any of these ways. That is just as true for pastors' children as it is for others.

Christians are forgiven people, and forgiven people forgive. Have you ever stopped to consider how serious and even dangerous the Lord's Prayer is? We pray, "Forgive us our debts, as we forgive our debtors" (Matt. 6:12). To make sure that we do not miss the point, Jesus adds, "For if you forgive men their trespasses, your heavenly Father will also forgive you. But if you do not forgive men their trespasses, neither will your Father forgive your trespasses" (vv. 14–15).

Jesus wasn't saying that we earn God's forgiveness by forgiving others. Rather, He was acknowledging the truth that forgiven sinners forgive. Think of what you are actually praying in the Lord's Prayer if you refuse to forgive people who have sinned against you. If you are living in unforgiveness, do you really want the Lord to forgive you in the same way that you have forgiven others?

One of the benefits that comes from living in a covenanted relationship with a church is the many opportunities that you will have to forgive. When sinners (redeemed sinners, yes, but nevertheless people with sin still remaining in them) unite in a local church to live as the family of God, they will inevitably sin against each other at times. This is why we must learn to live in forgiveness.

This is what Peter had in mind when he wrote, "Above all things have fervent love for one another, for 'love will cover a multitude of sins'" (1 Peter 4:8). Learning to love the church goes hand in hand with learning to be a quick forgiver.

So often we are tempted to hold grudges and nurse the wounds we have received through the words or actions of others. Yet that way of living is contrary to the very nature of the gospel that has saved us. At the heart of our salvation is forgiveness. God has not held our sins against us but has completely forgiven us for the sake of all that Jesus accomplished in His life, death, and resurrection.

Having been forgiven, we also must forgive. This is what Paul tells the church at Ephesus (and the other churches whom he intended to read his letter). "Be kind to one another, tenderhearted, forgiving one another, even as God in Christ forgave you" (Eph. 4:32). The foundation of our forgiveness of others is God's forgiveness of us in Christ. As C. S. Lewis reminds us, "To be a Christian means to forgive the inexcusable because God has forgiven the inexcusable in you."

Forgiveness is always costly. That is why Jesus put it in terms of debt in the Lord's Prayer. To forgive a debt is to absorb the cost yourself. It is to release the debtor from making a payment. That is exactly what Jesus has done for His people. He paid the debt that we owe due to our sin. We are no longer held liable for it. We are free. Forgiven.

When we forgive those who sin against us, we no longer hold their sin against them. This does not mean that we pretend they did not sin or that their sin has not been hurtful. In fact, if the sin has been serious enough (so that it doesn't fall into the category mentioned in 1 Peter 4:8), your forgiveness will need to be matched by their repentance in order for genuine, two-sided reconciliation to take place.

It is helpful to remember that you can extend forgiveness to those who have sinned against you without trusting them. Forgiveness and trust don't necessarily come at the same time. Forgiveness can be extended before trust is reestablished. Perhaps in time and by God's grace, trust will be restored in the relationship, but if not, you can still extend grace and forgiveness to those who have hurt you.

If God has forgiven us of our sins against Him, we must forgive others when they sin against us. We find strength and motivation to do so when we keep in mind just how much we have been forgiven. This is the point of Jesus's parable in Matthew 18:21–35. A king forgave his servant a debt of billions of dollars, only to have that servant turn around and refuse to forgive a debt of several thousand dollars. When the king found out about it, he called his servant to appear before him. This is what he said: "You wicked servant! I forgave you all that debt because you begged me. Should you not also have had compassion on your fellow servant, just as I had pity on you?" (vv. 32–33).

Jesus concluded the story by saying, "His master was angry, and delivered him to the torturers until he should pay all that was due to him. So My heavenly Father also will do to you if each of you, from his heart, does not forgive his brother his trespasses" (vv. 34–35). If we refuse to forgive, then we must examine ourselves and ask if we have genuinely experienced God's forgiveness of our sins through Jesus Christ.

That is a sobering thought, but it will help you to fight against harboring unforgiveness against others. No one ever has or ever could sin against us more than we have sinned against God. Our sins against Him—affronts to His goodness, holiness, and innocence—are far greater than any sins committed against us. And through Christ, He has forgiven our greater sins against Him. Therefore, through that very grace that we have received, we are able to forgive others their lesser sins against us.

Sometimes that is easier to do when you have been sinned against directly than when you have watched a fellow church member sin against your parents. To forgive them can feel like disloyalty to your mom and dad. It can seem as though you are treating sin lightly.

Such feelings are real, and our own children have admitted to having them at times. Though it was not always easy, they often talked to us about those inner struggles. Those conversations, though difficult, were helpful.

We encourage you to talk to your mom and dad about those internal battles when they arise. Your parents love you, and they have to fight the same fight in their own souls and can help you remember how the gospel works in such trials. As you do this, the Lord will cause your faith to grow in such ways that you, in turn, will be able to help others (including your parents) in their own fight of faith. That has certainly been our experience, and we have often been encouraged in this way by our own children.

If you are going to love the church as you ought and enjoy all the benefits that God intends by calling us to live faithfully in a church, then you are going to have to grow in developing a forgiving disposition. That is, you must cultivate an attitude of being always ready to forgive anyone who sins against you.

This disposition is far more important than we often realize. Chuck Swindoll offers some helpful counsel here:

> The longer I live, the more I realize the impact of attitude on life. Attitude to me is more important than facts, it's more important that the past.... It's more important than what other people think or say or do. It's more important than appearance, giftedness, or skill. It will make or break a company, a church, or a home. The remarkable thing is that we have a choice every day regarding the attitude we will embrace. We cannot change our past. We cannot change the fact that people will act in a certain way. We cannot change the inevitable. The only thing we can do is play on the one string that we have, and that is our attitude. I'm convinced that life is ten percent of what happens to me and ninety percent of how I react to it.

Fighting for the right attitude is critical to forgiveness in any church and home, but it is especially important in a pastor's home. As we have already mentioned, your parents have flaws. Some pastors have very deep flaws. Sadly, as we know from experience, pastors sin against their children. This is inevitable. Sometimes, it can be very painful. As a Christian child of a pastor, you must not only honor him as your father but also learn to live in repentance and forgiveness with him as your brother in the Lord. The grace that we have received in Christ is powerful enough to enable you to do this.

If things ever get so difficult in your relationship with your parent or parents, you should consider seeking counsel from a trusted elder or other respected member of the church. If that seems unfeasible, then ask for help from some other respected Christian outside the church. Whatever you do, do not let unresolved conflicts gnaw away at you. Ask for help. Do not be afraid to speak truthfully about tensions in your relationships at home. Our God raises people from the dead, and He is able and willing to help sort out any problem that arises because of sin.

Conclusion

Above all, in the midst of the hurt that can come by living life with other broken, redeemed sinners, remember that Christ is not indifferent to the church. He loves the church, He gave His life for the church, and He will one day "present her to Himself a glorious church, not having spot or wrinkle or any such thing, but that she should be holy and without blemish" (Eph. 5:27). As a child of God, you are called to love the church for the sake of Christ.

Charles Spurgeon wisely notes that "the Church is not an institution for perfect people, but a sanctuary for sinners saved by Grace, who, though they are saved, are still sinners and need all the help they can derive from the sympathy and guidance of their fellow Believers. The Church is the nursery for God's weak children where they are nourished and grow strong. It is the fold for Christ's sheep—the home for Christ's family."

We are all God's weak children who need a place to grow in grace and holiness. Don't give up on the church! Don't run from those for whom Jesus has spilled His blood. Rather, seek to love and serve and grow together with fellow brothers and sisters who are on this journey of grace with you.

Settle it early in your Christian pilgrimage that to know and follow Jesus is to live in a loving, devoted relationship to His body, the church. Discipline yourself to remember that all that you are and anything that you attain are due to God's grace poured out on you because of Jesus Christ. So live by grace, and look for the evidences of grace in the life of your church. When you see them, remember that God is working among His people, and be encouraged.

Warmly,

Tom and Donna Ascol

Tom and Donna Ascol got married in 1980, while Tom was pastoring his first church in College Station, Texas, and Donna was completing a BS in nursing. Since 1986 they have lived in Cape Coral, Florida, where Tom serves as senior pastor of Grace Baptist Church. He is also the president of Founders Ministries. The Ascols have five daughters (three of whom are married) and a married son. They love watching their twelve grandchildren (with another due this year) grow up in the church.

PART 2

SHARKS IN THE BOWL

CRITICISM
The Godly Response

Mike and Mae Milton

I have seen firsthand what criticism can do to a pastor and his family. Over the course of a ministry, every pastor receives more than his fair share of harsh critique, baseless accusation, manipulative hint-dropping, and hurtful blame shifting from members of their congregation, and sometimes even from their elders and deacons. This was certainly the case with my dad. In my mind's eye, which is no doubt colored by a son's love and respect, I always remember him responding thoughtfully, prayerfully, with an open Bible spread out before him. I witnessed his soul weighed down with pain, as though an iron ball were chained to his heart with razor wire. Watching him taught me many things: when pain abounded, grace abounded much more. When men failed Dad, God stood with him. And through it all he became more than a conqueror in Christ. Over the course of time, God helped me resist the manifold temptations toward bitterness, and I grew to love both the Lord and His bride, the church. I came to realize that the church is a family of flawed sinners. We are great sinners, to be sure, but we have a far greater Savior. As you read this letter, whatever criticism might be coming down the pike at you, I pray that God will give you the same testimony and that you will learn to build your identity upon the eternal love of Christ and not on the passing criticisms of mortal men.

Your fellow PK,

John Michael Ellis Milton

Dear Pastor's Kid,

I hope you are growing into a fine young child of the King. It is our earnest prayer for you that you might mature in both faith and stature, and that you will learn to walk through the garden gate of Christ's family, realizing all of God's goodness for you in the church at large.

Growing up in a pastor's home usually involves finding yourself on the business end of some of the "slings and arrows" that other families miss. Of course, we also receive peculiar blessings others don't enjoy—so it's not all bad news! But whatever the case, both the blessing and the bane of ministry life revolve around *people*: the people we serve for Christ's sake as a pastoral family.

There are, in this fallen world, certain spiritual strains of *human viruses*—disorders of the soul—that can infect us. If these infections go untreated, they can hurt us for a lifetime. But the Lord has provided a way to address even the most virulent of these through His Word and Spirit. I want to write to you about one of the most toxic of these diseases: *criticism*—not only *how to deal with it* but *how to handle the enduring pain it can leave deep inside.* Sadly, such pain is an almost unavoidable piece of baggage children of the manse must carry with them through their life.

The process of growing up is like climbing a ladder. In our youth, we often fancy this ladder will soon come to an end, but it actually continues throughout our life. Each new phase of our development brings with it a fresh ladder to climb. The path forward is always upward. I am still climbing the ladder of life, though the dark-haired minister in old photographs has long since been replaced with the frosty cap of those who have begun to climb above the snowline of life's journey.

In life, as with other forms of climbing, "Don't look down" is good advice. Paul says as much in his letter to the Philippians: "But one thing I do, forgetting those things which are behind and reaching forward to those things which are ahead" (Phil. 3:13). Sometimes, however, we forget this advice and look down at the dizzying slopes below. The old faces, figures of foggy memory, and the scenes—long since forgotten—come flooding in, and we see our lives replaying down in that overgrown, deserted mine in the valley. We thought we had left the wounds and the ache all behind. Yet now, what we see below us, behind us, is inevitably the upsetting experiences, the cruel memories. We realize, at that moment, that we have been climbing *away* from something (or someone), just as much, or more, than we have been climbing *toward* something. Should that happen—and it happens to each of us in one way or another, for there are few of us who get out of this life without the pockmarks of pain—*we are no longer climbing.* We are *frozen*—frozen with fear and hanging on the ladder for dear life. The thing is, dear Christian, that some people go through life never climbing further than the first time they stopped climbing to look back. I have counseled them; I have applied Word, sacrament, and prayer to bring healing to them. Many return to climbing the ladder of life. Others struggle, stuck in the misty flats betwixt and between progress for the rest of their lives.

One such thing that can leave PKs frozen with fright on the ladder of progress is criticism. On a side note, it is interesting that Mae, my wife, who is also a "Pastor's Kid," does not remember such criticism coming at her father or her family. Mae says, "So many of our parishioners were farmers and were too busy in the fields to be overly concerned with our family doing this or that. It was also a different time in the American Midwest [in the 1960s]. The clergy were respected in small towns and were depended on so much." I think the fact that Mae doesn't remember criticism of her dad or any of her family is really a tribute to her mother and her father, who more than likely kept any criticism away from their daughters. But when such criticism comes, it can be one of the most painful experiences in life and can be the kind that lodges, like the dreaded deer tick, in the folds of our soul, stuck there, infecting the entire ecosystem of our spiritual lives, depositing its foul disease within our spirits.

In dealing with criticism, we must be clear. The criticism itself is not really the danger. It is how we handle the criticism that almost always causes the real damage to our hearts. Let's say, for example, that your Sunday school teacher (or perhaps an elder, or someone you didn't even know) criticized your dad in a most unkind manner. Perhaps they even added in some gossip for good measure when they criticized your father. And you, let's say, somehow heard all about it. How did you feel? Well, of course, it hurt you. But worse, it hurt your father and your mother very deeply indeed. In my experience, this is often the key element. If Mom or Dad is able to take the negative word in their stride, often the children manage to continue their climb upward relatively unfazed. But when the blow hits home, and we see Dad discouraged, or, worse still, Mom shedding tears over the wound, that's generally when children find themselves unraveling.

At such times, it is easy for the family to allow the criticism to consume them. You know the kind of thing: talking endlessly about it at breakfast, rehearsing the pain in the evening at the dinner table, brooding over it on the way to football/ piano practice, picking at the scab on the way to youth group. We have all done this. Even when Dad tries to bottle it all up, to absorb the sharp edge of the words into his own soul, his wife will almost always know something is up, and the children do as well. Most PK parents never can discover that perfect mask to conceal their feelings. In some sense, though, I think we like it that way. Hiding is acting, and being too good of an actor is a dangerous skill in both life and ministry. It tends to destroy intimacy, which is at least in part the safest and only pathway through the pain such criticism causes.

How Should We Respond?

My wife, Mae, was a master at this. Mae had this wonderful habit of taking the cutting, crushing words and leaving them, and the people who spoke them, at the "foot of the cross," leaving her burden with our Lord Jesus, as many folks have heard me preach. I, on my part, had the unhappy habit of holding on to the words and the pain they caused. Too often I brought it all home, and like a dark cloud it followed me around, watering the seed of bitterness, nourishing it into a stinkweed threatening to consume not only my ministry but also my heart and Christian testimony.

By God's grace, however, where sin abounds the Lord's grace doth much more abound. And time and again the Spirit of the living God would come through the Word (sometimes through sermons I myself was preaching!) and begin to root out these burning, hellish embers from my soul that were threatening to undo all He had done so far.

God Moves in a Mysterious Way

In the book of Proverbs, we find these mysterious words: "The preparations of the heart belong to man, but the answer of the tongue is from the LORD" (Prov. 16:1). Without in any way undermining our responsibility for what we say (Matt. 12:36), Solomon seems to have been saying that God has a purpose behind every word we say, and, by implication, this purpose is good (Rom. 8:28). Like the pain-relieving gel Mother used to rub onto bee stings, remembering this can help calm the sharp sting of unkind criticism. God always has a lesson for us to learn, if we have ears to hear. Our gracious and wise Savior has a wonderful way of healing people through their wounds. One thing is for certain: pain never leaves us the same—always better or worse, but never the same. As we choose how to respond, very often we choose which path we will take—up for the better or down for the worse.

Pray for Your Enemies

Another important secret in responding to criticism is to bring not only our wounds to Jesus but also those who wounded us in the first place. We must pray for them. Such prayer very often has a wonderfully melting effect upon our own hearts, opening them up and enabling us to let go of the pain, to dissolve the bitterness, and to offer forgiveness at an appropriate time (Matt. 5:44; Luke 17:3; 1 Peter 2:21–25). This is the pathway to joy and inner peace. I think of the words that St. Paul wrote to embattled believers in the church at Rome:

> Beloved, do not avenge yourselves, but rather give place to wrath; for it is written, "Vengeance is Mine, I will repay," says the Lord. Therefore
> "If your enemy is hungry, feed him;
> If he is thirsty, give him a drink;
> For in so doing you will heap coals of fire on his head."
> Do not be overcome by evil, but overcome evil with good.
> (Rom. 12:19–21)

If you were to do nothing more with this letter than to meditate on those infallible and inerrant words from the former Chief Critic and Persecutor himself—Saul of Tarsus—you not only would find your healing from any pain of the past but would find your strength to climb upward through every strong wind of resistance; every reproach; every hostile lie, rumor, and innuendo ever spoken against you. God's Word is sufficient to protect, to heal, to comfort, and to guide.

Remember, Remember

1. Hurting people hurt others: many of those individuals who heap hurt on you are, frequently, the sufferer of some crisis of existential torment themselves. They are to be pitied, not hated.

2. Sinners have a habit of sinning (that includes us). The best member of the church is a recovering pagan at best. To be sure, the most powerful force in the universe is at work in us both to will and to do for His good pleasure, but we still have the terrible propensity of making foolish mistakes, of saying stupid things, and sometimes even of deploying spiteful, insensitive words aimed at cutting others to the core. "There is one," Solomon says, "who speaks like the piercings of a sword, but the tongue of the wise promotes health" (Prov. 12:18). I often wonder at my capacity for personifying both parts of this verse, if not at the same moment, then certainly on the same day. Why we intentionally devise cunning conspiracies to employ our tongues as instruments of our own embittered spirits to slice and dice each other, who are closest to us, remains one of the mysteries of this fallen world. In his epistle James told us about these things, though, didn't he? "Out of the same mouth proceed blessing and cursing. My brethren, these things ought not to be so" (James 3:10). Indeed, these things ought not to be, but the Bible confirms that they are. It is unquestionably true that unfair criticism seems to be more easily bestowed than deserving praise.

3. Even a broken clock is right twice a day: sometimes our "enemies" can nail us in the right place for the wrong reason. There is a lesson to be learned here, though, isn't there! Mae and I have learned that when we receive criticism we must remain alert, not switch off because it lacks the delight of "good news from a far country" that we might prefer. Someone said that "honest criticism is particularly hard to take, especially from a relative, friend, co-worker, acquaintance, or stranger."

Ah, truer words have never been spoken! Does that possibly leave anyone out? Yet the Bible calls us to a better way:

Faithful are the wounds of a friend,
But the kisses of an enemy are deceitful. (Prov. 27:6)

Behold, happy is the man whom God corrects;
Therefore do not despise the chastening of the Almighty. (Job 5:17)

So, we must not immediately dismiss the one bearing criticism as "some *nutjob* trying to ruin my dad's ministry." Indeed, though they may have a personality disorder or other emotional problem, jealousy or bitter pride, sometimes the Lord uses such curious strategies to reach us. We must, therefore, pay attention to everything. We should listen to all (and, by the way, this also shows respect and common decency to the human being who is speaking to you, regardless of their own motivations; and this becomes a good and godly strategy to "heap burning coals on his head"—to repay kindness for injury and, therefore, engender goodwill). Only after careful listening do we then gather the criticism and quickly bring it, undiluted, unfiltered—not over-analyzed—to the Lord in humble prayer. There, before the Lord, leave the matter with Him.

Search me, O God, and know my heart;
Try me, and know my anxieties;
And see if there is any wicked way in me,
And lead me in the way everlasting. (Ps. 139:23–24)

To leave the matter with the Lord entrusts both the critic and the criticism to the Almighty to "sort through." This is good and right for your own soul, and such a process allows for time to pass, respecting the one who brought the criticism. In this way, you wait on the Lord to show you, through Scripture, through the power of the Holy Spirit working through your own spirit, and through holy providence whether that criticism is (1) valid, and thus you need to remedy your ways; (2) partially valid, and, perhaps, you need to attend to your wayward heart and less-than-pure motivations; or (3) invalid, and possibly a result of the person's ongoing process of sanctification (a matter that may be of interest to you if you were his or her pastor, but otherwise is, certainly and foremost, the business of God and that person). Of course, there really is a *fourth* response. The person could indeed be a "wolf" or, to use a metaphor from an old pastoral theology book I read in seminary, one of the "congregational dragons" unwittingly stationed by the "Old Dragon" of Revelation 12:9 to devour pastors and pastoral families. But you will never know which of these four conditions is present before you; you will never discern one from the other; and you will, certainly, never demonstrate godly patience, humility, and honor to others by rushing in to answer a criticism with an angry or defensive reaction. You must, first, listen. Then, take it to the Lord in prayer. Leave it with Him for a while. Then you must wait patiently on His answer. Assess His response to you. Obediently follow Him. Finally, correct your ways, if that is the Lord's leading and the conviction in your soul, and, if necessary, forgive the critic, or merely "fret not" any more about it. And pray that the Lord would keep you from evil company and give you good and godly company.

Now, after a lifetime of ministry, that is how Mae and I seek to handle criticism in the church. As I have confessed, we have not always done it perfectly. But, if the Lord has brought about any good, any happiness in our home—and I testify that our family life has been the joy that has fueled my pastorate—then, know that it is because, at least in part, we have followed the Lord in this vital area of relationships. The larger result of this biblical approach to criticism in the ministry is that we can live together in the community of the faithful without having to always leave that particular ministry every time uncomfortable words are said and feelings are bruised. This happens all too often in the church. The walking wounded roam from parish to parish in search of the perfect pastor and the perfect church that will heal the pain in their lives that only God can cure and only forgiveness will activate. Life together, to borrow from the Dietrich Bonhoeffer title, is not an idealized community of people who have arrived at a state of spiritual perfection. Far from it! It is, rather, like the disciples themselves: a God-chosen collection of broken-down people on their way to becoming what God has ordained them to be from the foundation of the world. In any given congregation, different people are at different points along the continuum of spiritual progress. We are *together* because a great part of how God makes us into the image of Christ *requires* the living dynamic of forgiveness that comes only from such a community.

Alright, then. We have laid out "how to handle criticism" for you. Yet you still may find, sometimes, that an old memory, an old wound stops you in your tracks along the way, inhibits your scaling the ladder of life. When you experience that ache or when you come to some other sad occasion to look down at painful memories left behind, the way out of the paralysis of anxiety is the confession, "Lord, Jesus, you are sovereign. Father, as I have been forgiven through your Son, Jesus, so I forgive." Remember, too, the model of St. Paul: "Brethren, I do not count myself to have apprehended; but one thing I do, forgetting those things which are behind and reaching forward to those things which are ahead, I press toward the goal for the prize of the upward call of God in Christ Jesus" (Phil. 3:13–14).

Then turn your head upward. Look up to the goals before you. Stretch out your arm for the next rung on the ladder of life. And let the rich experiences of your childhood as the "child of the manse" nourish you in your faith. Leave criticism with the Lord and see whether there is anything to it. Leave the critics with the Lord because they are His to tend. You just lift your head back up. Look to the next rung on the ladder.

And climb, dear child of the King, climb.

Your fellow laborer in the gospel,

Mike

Michael A. Milton, PhD (Wales), is an emeritus Presbyterian minister (PCA, ARP) whose record of service includes pastor, educator, army chaplain (colonel), author, and composer. Dr. Milton is the provost of Erskine Seminary and president of the D. James Kennedy Institute. An alumnus of UNC–Chapel Hill, he and his wife, Mae, reside in North Carolina.

LONELINESS
Friendship in Solitary Seasons

Amanda Martin

Here are words of hope for every PK struggling with loneliness (and words of comfort for every PK parent!). Amanda has known loneliness and describes it compellingly. Her experience makes her a wise and sympathetic traveling companion for those walking the same solitary path.

To read our daughter's testimony is to flirt afresh with the fears of every PK parent. How reassuring to find that our heavenly Father cares more passionately for His children than any earthly parent! In her travels, Amanda has discovered fair flowers of paradise blooming even in shadowy places. Her words breathe out their sweet fragrance—filled with hope springing from the Scriptures that she, like Timothy, has both known from infancy and made her own. Here, too, are the cheering voices of the saints of old, drawing us back into fellowship with renewed vision and hope. Amanda translates her insights and theirs into sound practical advice so that we are emboldened by the Lord's own comforting companionship and equipped to bring that comfort to others (2 Cor. 1:3–4).

Warmly,
Rev. Tom and Trish Martin

Dear PK,

It is an honor to write to you—and, to my surprise, it is difficult as well. As I've thought about how to tackle this subject, I've wondered about *you*—if you're happy to be a PK or if you're unhappy, if you feel lonely sometimes, as everyone does, or if loneliness is the persistent, defining trouble in your life right now.

I don't know you. But since we share the PK label, we must share more than that. Are your weeks shaped by church activities? Do people expect you to know all the answers in Sunday school? (Or maybe teach Sunday school?) Does the whole congregation seem to know your birthday? Do you know when something serious is happening at church, not because your father says anything in particular but because of those other clues? Do you feel somehow set apart from your peers, even isolated?

Loneliness is a painful part of many people's lives. For PKs, the factors contributing to our loneliness may be specifically tied to our parents' position. It's very possible, as a PK, to feel alienated from the church community or to become cut off from your peers. Even being introduced as the "pastor's kid" is isolating if people make assumptions about you. You may be held up by parents in the congregation as a "good kid" and a model for their own children (which is awkward). Or your situation may be more severe: you may experience unconstructive criticism or rejection from the people around you.

Writing about loneliness is difficult because loneliness genuinely alarms me. Years ago I confessed to a woman at church that I was lonely, only to be told that I'd better get used to it! Ever since then, a little loneliness in the today has felt like the promise of loneliness forever—inevitable and irreversible.

It's not, though. There's plenty of hope out there, for you and me both.

What Is Loneliness, Anyway?

Loneliness is defined by *lack*. Something isn't there.

"We are full of things that impel us outwards," Blaise Pascal wrote in his *Pensées*. "Our instinct makes us feel that our happiness must be sought outside ourselves." Ultimately, our only true, lasting happiness comes from a relationship with God. But God in His generosity has created us to need other things besides Himself, and He has given us instincts to prod us toward those things. When we need food, we get hungry. When we need water, we get thirsty. When our reasonable, appropriate desire to engage with other people is unmet, we get lonely.

As with any thwarted desire, loneliness can be difficult to handle well. It can become a driving or destructive force in our lives. You'll know this especially if you are bombarded by despairing thoughts, such as, *This is forever. You can't bear this. No one likes you. You don't matter. There's nothing you can do.* The truth is much better than that: This is a momentary affliction. You are beloved. God will give you the strength you need to handle this—and so much more than you can even imagine.

Though our tolerance for solitude may vary, we all need people. We need relationships, but we don't always have them. What do we do in the meantime?

In writing this letter, I don't want to place new burdens on you. It's easy to feel as though you are to blame for your own loneliness, and that's often not the case. Plus, as a PK, you may already experience a lot of pressure to engage with people. That doesn't always help! So, as you read on, please remember that if you are weary and heavy laden, Jesus Christ will give you rest (Matt. 11:28). You can approach your loneliness from a place of peace and soul-safety, not guilt, panic, or desperation.

First Things First: Look to God

When I was young, I had all the friends I wanted. I love my memories of playing tag or catching fireflies with them on summer nights after the evening service. But their families moved away as time went on. When I was in eighth grade, my family started homeschooling. During my high school years, my brother, sister, and I said goodbye to all but one of our church and school friends.

But I experienced loneliness in a truly concentrated dose when I moved away from home postcollege. I lived in a new state, in a town unfamiliar to me, alone in a trailer on a hill. It took me a while to find a church. It took longer for me to make any local friends I saw regularly. As an introvert, I thought I was okay coming home from work and curling up with a book or washing my dishes. I would feel fine (so independent and self-sufficient!) until the loneliness hit with a tangible sense of panic. Instead of galvanizing me to reach out to people, loneliness paralyzed me.

Loneliness also pushed me toward God—sometimes. Not always. But during my hermit days I learned that no time spent with Him is ever wasted. When we're lonely, the instinct is to distract ourselves away from the loneliness, and going to God with all our sin and bad feelings requires acknowledging what we may prefer to deny. It doesn't seem that facing all that mess head-on will actually help, but it does.

Adam and Eve, two perfect human beings in a perfect paradise, needed a close and loving relationship with God to make their joy complete. Like them, we were made to be fulfilled by our relationship with our Maker. We need God, and the wonderful thing about needing God is that we can have Him: He is the friend of "those who fear Him" (Ps. 25:14), and He assures us that He remains near to those who call on Him (Ps. 145:18).

Our relationship is of such extreme value and importance that when it was broken God Himself, fully human in the person of His Son, suffered and died to restore it. There is no greater love—in heaven or on earth or under the earth—than the unflinching, uncompromising love God has extended to us in friendship.

As a PK, you may wonder who really knows, and likes, the real you. Your father may use you in sermon illustrations, creating a flattering or unflattering picture of you that informs your public persona at church. Your family may often move to new churches, so that it's hard to put down roots and get to know people. You may feel that your help at church is assumed rather than appreciated. You may be encouraged to avoid making special friends in the congregation but to be a friend to all. Who sees you? Who cares?

If you feel overlooked or invisible, remember that if you are God's child, you are loved by the God who sees you (Gen. 16:13). God is well known for remembering forgotten people: Joseph, Hannah, and the enslaved Israelites in Egypt, to name a few. David wrote: "You number my wanderings; put my tears into Your bottle; are they not in Your book?" (Ps. 56:8). God is your witness, and He is keeping a record.

And He doesn't leave it there! Unlike those who watch from a distance, Christ "carried our sorrows" (Isa. 53:4). He is not turned off by your pain and dismay, or even by your neediness. God Himself has experienced suffering, understands your suffering, and is compassionate toward you. Because your sins are forgiven through Christ's work, He never stands in judgment of you.

The slave girl Hagar realized that not only had God seen her but she had seen Him (Gen. 16:13). God sees you and cares for you—and there will be evidence of that in your life. Are you looking for it? Some of my own profoundest experiences of loneliness and isolation have made me deeply aware of God's grace as it gets me through each day. It's a comfort to remember in the morning, "When I awake, I am still with You" (Ps. 139:18). God is present in our loneliness.

God also draws us into community, starting with His Trinity. Many books, TV shows, and movies feature a lone main character who is befriended seemingly out of nowhere by an exuberant person who draws him or her into a whole group of friends. It's great to watch the protagonist blossom in their company. But Jesus's promise is infinitely greater: "If anyone loves Me, he will keep My word; and My Father will love him, and We will come to him and make Our home with him" (John 14:23). Your body is indeed a temple of the Holy Spirit (1 Cor. 6:19), but our triune God is close and personal. God is going out of His way to make His *home* with you, to live with you in intimate proximity.

The psalmist wrote, "In the multitude of my anxieties within me, Your comforts delight my soul" (Ps. 94:19). God "will never leave you nor forsake you" (Heb. 13:5). As the poet Gerard Manley Hopkins put it, Jesus is your "ransom, [your] rescue, and first, fast, last friend." He's not going away.

Do you know your friend? One way to assess this is to ask another question: Are you trusting God right now? The discomfort I feel in my loneliness reflects my uncertainty with God. I doubt that He's enough for me. I doubt that He is with me. I doubt that He is working good in my life. In *Help My Unbelief: Why Doubt Is Not the Enemy of Faith*, Barnabas Piper writes, "The deeper we go in relationship with [God], the greater our trust grows…. In relationship with Him we see daily His complete trustworthiness, goodness, power, and presence. We are never left alone or abandoned by Him. He never gives us reason to doubt Him." A close relationship with God comforts us because it pushes against our doubt.

How do we get to a close relationship? You can probably predict my answers, so I'll be brief.

Start with the Bible. Piper says it well: "In a relationship, we enjoy hearing from those we love and we are energized and helped by them, even if what they have to say is a hard word for us. We love to converse, exchange texts or emails, and spend time with loved ones. That is Scripture, God's correspondence and conversation with us. It is our way to spend time with Him." When we read God's Word, it shapes us in ways we don't even realize, speaking to our hearts through the Holy Spirit. This is our primary way to get to know God.

God's Word starts the conversation. We participate through prayer. Do you pray before you read the Bible, asking God for understanding? Do you go to God afterward with your response, whatever that may be? God delights to hear from you. You may pray in bursts throughout the day—in moments of alarm or thanksgiving, delight or distress. The psalms describe prayers in the early morning and prayers through the night. Our prayers make us mindful of God's presence. He is close enough to hear.

I like to sing, and I particularly like to sing hymns. You may not. But I have found hymns very helpful. When I'm not sure how to pray—if I can't find the words, the thoughts, the feelings—singing is straightforward. Many hymns refer to God's friendship, from the old favorite "What a Friend We Have in Jesus" to John Newton's more obscure "One There Is, Above All Others" to the hymn of pure comfort "Be Still, My Soul" by Katharina A. von Schlegel. It's a scavenger hunt! If you like to sing, try exploring a hymnal (or a praise book or an album) and making it your own.

There's so much to say here, but I'd like to hit a few other points before I conclude.

Remember to Look Out for Others

We look *to* God because our relationship with Him is foundational. The Heidelberg Catechism begins by emphasizing that our only comfort in life and death is that we are not our own but belong to Jesus. The thing is, that little word *only* is hard to believe. You will not find your comfort in people, although they are a blessing. You can't put all your confidence in them or make them the foundation of your hope. But you can still love them (and you should!). And the way to start loving them is to look out for them.

When you're feeling unhappy for whatever reason, it's easy to get caught up in that unhappiness. When loneliness makes us feel needy or vulnerable, our instinct can be to withdraw, to wait for other people to prove we matter by being the first to make an approach. Ironically, we can focus on our need for other people and forget that other people need *us*.

Other people need us particularly (but not exclusively) in the church. Describing God's people as a body, Paul points out, "The eye cannot say to the hand, 'I have no need of you'; nor again the head to the feet, 'I have no need of you'" (1 Cor. 12:21). According to Paul, even the "members of the body which seem to be weaker are necessary" (v. 22). The eye, hand, head, and feet all play their part in serving God, but they are also necessary to one another.

I was blessed to grow up in a church in which many people were very supportive of my family, some even praying for us daily. I knew everyone by name and could start a conversation with anyone in the congregation. I was surprised by how strange it felt, when I moved away from my father's church, to attend churches in which I was not the pastor's daughter. I missed being known by people and having an insider's view (limited as it was) of what was going on. I hadn't fully realized that I had been in a "special" position until I no longer was.

Do you realize how much you matter? Not because you're a PK, or because you're a model of good Christian [fill in the blank], or because you can be counted on to volunteer for this or that church thing. You matter because you are part of Christ's body, and you have something to offer for the very same reason. In *Made for More: An Invitation to Live in God's Image*, author Hannah Anderson gets to the heart of it: God Himself is "working through us to care for His world."

On a practical level, if you are lonely, you are probably becoming gifted to reach out to other lonely people. If you notice that a member of the congregation hasn't been able to come to church due to illness or another difficulty, consider sending them a note. If you're in a position to babysit for a mother of young children so that she can get out of the house, try that. If you see people standing by themselves after a worship service, say hi. It feels almost cold-bloodedly pious to write this, and I don't do so to add an item to your to-do list, but don't let waiting for other people to get to know you stop you from looking for people to know and serve. Don't let your pain make it hard to see them.

To take this in another direction, Paul's point about the body gives you the freedom to pursue friendship with people who don't seem like your usual type. Your father's job may turn you into a stranger in an unfamiliar culture—a suburbanite in an urban setting, a foreigner in a new country, a racial or ethnic minority, a lone homeschooler or Christian schooler or public schooler. Your pastor-father may work in a church with very few others your age. But eyes who only hang out with other eyes miss out on the joys of fellowshipping with hands and feet. When my siblings and I made up most of the young people in our church, our parents encouraged us to get to know everyone else. I haven't regretted that. You may find friends who are significantly older or younger than you or who have had very different life experiences. In some cases, they may not seem to be the most desirable friends or to have much to offer you, but they, too, are indispensable.

Loneliness easily leads to discontent with the people around us. As we look out for others, we look out for the best in them rather than dwelling on their failings and insufficiencies. Are they kind? Wise? Well meaning? Have you seen them keep peace in a hostile situation or slow down to help someone? Jesus said, "Let your light so shine before men, that they may see your good works and glorify your Father in heaven" (Matt. 5:16). The people around you bear the image of God. They are *worth* knowing. Look for that light.

Finally, God has made you His ambassador in this particular place and for this particular time. When your father was called to a church, God called you to go with him. He didn't just have a plan for your father; he had a plan for you. Your loneliness may make you feel that you are not achieving your full potential. Your circumstances may make you feel claustrophobic—shouldn't you be part of something bigger, doing something more? But God has placed you with the people He wants you to know and love at this time. We can learn from Abraham, as Alec Motyer writes in *Isaiah by Day*, "that the single, solitary individual is of great significance. Our solitariness imposes no limitation on the Lord; our faithfulness as single individuals is of the utmost importance to him." Even our smallest acts of service are used for much good in God's plan.

And Don't Forget to Keep an Eye on Yourself, Too

Since my tendency is to forget God, look to others for my happiness, and look out for myself, I suppose I should be telling us both to look to God, look out for others, and forget ourselves. And, as Timothy Keller writes in *The Freedom of Self-Forgetfulness*, it's true that self-forgetfulness moves us away from pride or self-pity and makes way for a joyful life. But loneliness will get in our heads and tell us lies. We need to identify those lies and fight back—and this requires paying attention.

Years ago, someone gave me a birthday card that said, "Attitude is everything." I think about that a lot. Our attitude shapes the way we experience the world. Sometimes our attitude *becomes* our world. In *The Happy Christian*, Pastor David Murray points out that "most unhappy people are unhappy not because of their situation but because they let their feelings rule their thoughts, or they think about things in the wrong way." He describes a number of destructive thought patterns we can fall into, such as drawing extreme conclusions, focusing on the negative, and predicting bad outcomes. In our context, that might look like telling yourself, "I'm terrible at making friends. My loneliness is ruining my life. I'll be lonely forever." These thoughts become a steady background noise that wears us down before we realize what's going on.

If you have Jesus as your Friend and Lord and Brother and Savior, then despairing thoughts simply do not belong in your head. They are unwelcome intruders, and you need to defend yourself against them.

1. Start by identifying the false or persistent negative thoughts that come most naturally to you. I for one like to predict bad things, imagine how awful they will be (I have a pretty good imagination, unfortunately), and tell myself that I won't be able to handle them. I do this far more often than these things actually happen!

2. Identify what makes these thoughts so dangerous. They may be completely false, or they may distort the truth with an unnecessarily negative focus. On her *Housewife Theologian* blog, Aimee Byrd wrote, "Some of our tomorrows may be too much for us to handle today, but God will give us his comfort and strength *as we need it*" (emphasis added). She explains further that God doesn't give grace to deal with worst-case hypothetical scenarios. It's also hard to find strength to live with a lie ("No one likes me" or "Nothing I do even matters"). You need to know what is wrong about whatever you're thinking so that you can fight it with the truth. If you have not brought God into your thinking, you are on dangerous ground already.

3. Pay attention to what feeds your false thinking or your feelings of loneliness. Social media can be a great way to keep in touch with other people—or a great way to increase your loneliness as you watch other people's curated lives from a distance. Music is a gift from God, but not all music encourages positive or truth-focused thinking (not that you should listen only to upbeat music—but I for one have made the mistake of letting a bleak soundtrack to my life put me in a dark place). Certain books, shows, and movies may make you feel that you're missing out on the earthly relationships you need in order to solve all your problems. In short, the things you spend your time thinking and feeling strongly about will shape the way you think and feel—and that can either help or hurt! Pay attention to how they impact you, and then adjust your consumption of them accordingly.

4. Finally, "whatever things are true…whatever things are lovely, whatever things are of good report, if there is any virtue and if there is anything praiseworthy—meditate on these things" (Phil. 4:8). We reorient ourselves by remembering God and His gospel and by looking at the world around us with a clear-eyed, Christ-focused gaze. God assures us, "Fear not, for I am with you; be not dismayed, for I am your God. I will strengthen you, yes, I will help you, I will uphold you with My righteous right hand" (Isa. 41:10).

As a PK, your loneliness may be growing out of your own silence. Even if your parents are discreet, you may be aware of things going on within the church that you can't discuss with anyone else. Or you may have your own secrets. You may feel pressure (in your family, in your church) to behave, to reflect well on your parents, to not have any problems (the pastor has enough to deal with!). If your dad is preaching against sins that you've been committing in secret, if you find yourself having doubts about God or disagreements on certain issues, if you're developing thought or sin patterns that seem too weird, shameful, or alarming to share with anyone, these are difficult to bring to light.

In Ecclesiastes 4:10, the Teacher warns us, "Woe to him who is alone when he falls, for he has no one to help him up." We really do need people beside us. We may not be in physical danger, but it's easy to fall down a pit in our own minds or in our habits—and we need someone to pull us out, point us to God, and give us insights we can't find for ourselves. When we fall down, we need someone who knows where to look for us.

So, as you keep an eye on yourself, is there anyone you can invite to join you? If you have been keeping silent about something that is weighing on you and increasing your isolation, ideally you will be able to speak to your parents first. If you feel you can't, your father may be able to put you in touch with another pastor or elder. Is there a godly man or woman in the congregation who can dedicate some time to meeting with you? At this point, the goal is not so much to make a friend as to make an ally, someone who will fight alongside you.

As a PK, I saw how some people can take a lot of a pastor's time. I didn't want to be that person, and that pride led to unhelpful attempts at self-sufficiency. If you are honest with yourself and with others, you will be able to process your loneliness in a way that helps rather than harms you.

Better Get Used to It?

The woman at church who told me to get used to loneliness had a point: in an imperfect world, loneliness does come into our lives. It's hard, but it's not shocking. Still, I don't think we need to despair over it. You may be in a season of life when circumstances make it genuinely hard to develop good peer friendships, open up to people, or be vulnerable about your difficulties. Loneliness tells you that the season will last forever, but you can live in the hope of God's good provision for you. Loneliness insists that you can't handle your situation, but by God's grace you can. Loneliness whispers that your existence is less meaningful than it could be, but that is impossible. You may not be aware of the difference you are making, but God is using you, as His trusting son or daughter, to glorify Himself and to shine His light into the world. You are His delight.

Think of it this way: loneliness is defined by *lack*, but you are not defined by loneliness, even in your loneliest moments. In the movie *Toy Story*, Woody bases his whole identity not merely on the fact that he is a toy ("a child's plaything!") but on the fact that he belongs to a particular child, Andy. Indeed, Andy's name is written on his boot. If you are in a relationship with God, you can write on your hand "the LORD's" (Isa. 44:5)—not God's plaything but His friend. *That*, not your loneliness, is your true and lasting identity.

Though you may not have the relationships you long for right now, you are not defined by lack, either. The generosity of the triune God toward you is fathomless. God the Father has given you His Son, and, as Pastor Jack Miller said in *Saving Grace*, "when he gave his Son, there wasn't anything left that he had to give." His Son has told you, "I am with you always, even to the end of the age" (Matt. 28:20). His Holy Spirit guarantees that you will receive your inheritance (Eph. 1:13)—the joy and fullness of every promised blessing in Christ. There is no better comfort than that.

You can go forth with confidence—not empty, not needy, not lacking, but beloved, known, and secure.

Your sister,

Amanda

Amanda Martin is editorial director at P&R Publishing. She is a member of Trinity Orthodox Presbyterian Church in Easton, Pennsylvania, and enjoys trying and learning new things.

CULTURAL CHANGE
Adapting to New Surroundings

Carl and Catriona Trueman

In conjunction with the advice offered by my parents, it is also prudent to consider certain matters from the child's perspective. Although I have spent almost the entirety of my life in this country, those five formative years spent between England and Scotland have sometimes left me feeling apart and different from the community around me. We cannot pretend that an experience such as emigration does not present challenges or shape us. However, we must not resign ourselves to the belief that these experiences will be only traumatic and disturbing. Through family and faith, these difficulties strengthen us and bring us closer to the Lord.

I traveled safely through the skies to reach Philadelphia. However, at certain points the transition felt more like being left alone on a tattered ship with the role of guiding the vessel to safer waters resting upon my shoulders alone. I went to class alone, surrounded by unfamiliar faces who had grown up together on the playgrounds of Oreland. The hallways loomed before me, massive and intimidating sights for a boy accustomed to a tiny primary school in Scotland. I wondered often why my parents had removed me from those comforts, all I had ever known, and thrown me into this confusing land. I had traded in a land of bagpipes and kilts for a land of banjos and jeans.

While you will always find great strength through overcoming adversity, I would encourage you to remember that stormy waters will pass with time. Friends were made. My parents found community through church. I even bought a banjo. I was not alone on this ship after all, for the Lord had His eye on me at all times and looked after my best interests, just as my parents had all along.

There are certain things that will never change and you will never be able to control. My brother remains the boy whose three years of training on the pitches of Aberdeen have somehow given him a competitive advantage on the soccer field for his entire life. I am still the boy with the Viking blonde hair and the endearing but ultimately unintelligible accent. But beneath that blonde bunce, seared into my brain, lies a message that the emigration experience brought home to me: trust the Lord, for He has grand designs for you and will not let you err from that intended course.

Your fellow PK,
Peter Trueman

Dear Pastor's Kid,

It is hard sometimes, if not often, to understand the ways of the Lord, but we truly need to put our hope and confidence wholly in Him, as His ways are just and always right. While the Lord sees all things, we see only a little bit at a time, and so when we are called to do things that change our lives in dramatic ways, we can be tempted to worry or even to panic. Every one of us will face such moments at some point in our lives.

Such a moment came for us in the year 2001. That was when the Lord called us as a family to move not just from one town or city to another but from one country to another. It took a tremendous leap of faith on all of our parts.

Our family was living in Scotland, where all that our two precious children knew was village life; green, rolling hills; sand dunes; and the cold waters of the North Sea in Newburgh, Aberdeenshire. We were truly settled, or so we thought, as a family. John and Peter attended a small, rural village school, surrounded and loved by a wonderful church family in a church where the Word was faithfully preached and godly men and women cared for and delighted in them.

Consequently, when the Lord called us to move to the United States, it was not a decision we took lightly or made quickly. Uprooting happy children was not on our agenda. We prayerfully sought the Lord and trusted in His inerrant Word for guidance. This move was going to mean far more than just packing boxes and moving our household to a neighboring town. It meant uprooting both ourselves and our boys from all we knew and held dear. It meant removing our sons from all that was familiar: our beloved church; our culture; and, even more significantly, all our friends and loved ones.

Though our boys were young (John was seven and Peter five), we were careful to involve them in the process from the outset by being open with them about all the challenges that lay ahead. We told them that they would no longer be living in a small village, nestled in the hills near the coast, where everyone knew one another. They would have to adapt to a whole new culture and even exchange that Scottish brogue for a radically different accent! They would have to make new friends. They would have to embrace a new church and a new church family. The very thought of it was daunting. Yet we also told them that we knew from Scripture that we were not the first family who had ever moved. Throughout Scripture there are many instances where a family had to travel to a new land, and the journey could be difficult and even treacherous. In Bible times there were no modern means of transportation. Travel was slow and often dangerous. Compared to the journeys of the people in the Bible, ours would be comparatively safe and easy.

Of course, relatively few people have to move from one country to another. But many may still move from one town or city or state to another, and that too can be both exciting and terrifying. Moving from one continent to another is often no more daunting that moving from one state to another. To move in this way may not mean learning a new language, but whenever we leave friends and familiar places behind, we can be left confused and nervous. To be just a few hundred miles away from the people and places we know and love can sometimes seem as though we are on the other side of the world.

Our move to America was dramatic. It took us to a strange land far across the ocean. Of course, our feelings of anxiety and worry would be familiar to anyone who has ever moved away from their hometown. And it is not unlikely that you, too, may find yourself in such a scenario. If the Lord calls your parents to move even the shortest of distances from your hometown roots, the questions you will ask will be the same as our boys did. Will I be able to make new friends? Will they accept me? What will my new school be like? Will the teachers be kind to me? Will I be able to talk to the kids in my street about the love of Christ for me? What will our new church look like? Will I find new Christian boys and girls to hang out with after church? Will my church have a youth gathering during the week? Will Mom and Dad still have time to play with me, to listen to my worries, and to pray with me before I go to bed at night? These are credible questions and have been asked by all boys and girls whose parents have been called to minister in a new location.

It is encouraging, therefore, to remember that the Bible contains many stories of moves that were far more dramatic than just going to the next town or even to another country with the ease that we are all too familiar with today. Of course, in biblical times God's people didn't have the convenience of airplanes and boats. In Genesis 12, the Lord called Abraham to leave the land of Haran and go to Canaan. He left everything behind. Naturally, his mind was full of anxiety. It would not be a safe or easy journey but a long, arduous, and dangerous one. But the Lord was with him, as He had promised, and kept him safe, leading him to the new home that was planned for him from the beginning of all eternity. Later in that same book, Abraham's grandson Jacob went to Egypt to save his family from starvation during a famine. Can you imagine the anguish of such a departure? Staying at home meant death by starvation, but moving to a foreign land entailed unimaginable hurdles. Again, it would have been a long and dangerous trek through land inhabited by bandits and robbers. Consider also Paul in the New Testament. In the book of Acts, we are versed on his various missionary journeys. Paul suffered terribly on these journeys. Sometimes he was imprisoned, shipwrecked, or beaten. His travels were difficult and perilous. But through it all his confidence rested in the Lord, knowing that even his sufferings were part of God's plan and for God's glory.

Compared to the travels of these Bible characters, our move was going to be relatively easy, to a land that, though far away from home, was in many ways quite similar to our own. We wouldn't be pulled from our Westernized comfort, and yet it was still extremely far away from family and friends, from the only earthly resting place our children had ever known. It is in these types of moments that we realize how much stability is gained from familiarity. And we knew that we might never move back to Britain permanently. Our lives were about to be changed forever. Yet we still knew that one constant had not and would not change: the Lord. The Lord who had been faithful to His people in biblical times was still the same, and we could be confident that He would be as faithful in His care of us as He had been of a man such as Abraham.

Of course, we know from Scripture that the Lord is always with His children and always cares for them. He has promised us that He will never leave or forsake us. It doesn't matter whether we are emigrating to another country or simply moving to a town where we don't know anyone or have any friends. We can rest in God's loving and all-wise care for us. Having confidence in the sovereignty of God and knowing that His will is perfect gave us all, from the oldest to the youngest, great comfort and unfathomable peace of mind. There is not a single place on earth where God is not present and in control. His hand never loses a grip on us.

In the lead-up to the move, we were providentially able to visit Philadelphia, the place that would soon become our new hometown. This proved to be an immeasurable blessing in advance of our final journey. It was a welcome mercy from God's hand to see where we would be potentially living and where the boys would be going to school. While we didn't purchase a home during this visit, we did make a particular point of checking out the local neighborhoods and getting a feel for what our new daily life would look like. We also visited local schools. For our boys, this was high on their priority list, as it not only involved them in the process but also allowed us to hear their thoughts and understand how they were processing the enormity of such a move. It gave us a feel for those things that they considered important, things that might be a cause for concern or worry for them. We wanted them to know every detail of what was happening in an effort to inspire confidence in what we were doing.

This was important. When your mom and dad believe they are being called to move, you should ask them if you can go to see the place before the final move. It is always easier to move somewhere when you have some idea of what the place looks like, perhaps what house you'll be moving to, and even what bedroom you will be sleeping in. Maybe you might even be able to see the school that you'll be going to and get acquainted with some of the teachers who will be interacting with you on a daily basis. All of these little things are blessings from God and can help placate the upheaval over what is about to happen.

At such times, it is important to remember that the Lord cares for PKs and not just their parents! Though the move was precipitated by their father's job, our boys would be dramatically affected by it, with having to go to a new school and make new friends, as well as the other challenges of a new place. Sometimes when we are children it can seem that we hold less importance than our parents. This is especially so at moments when everything that is familiar is taken away. But children are inexpressibly important to God. Jesus welcomed the children and made it clear that the kingdom of heaven belongs to them (Matt. 19:14; Luke 18:16). Our heavenly Father cares for every age spectrum of His covenant children. Even at a young age, you can be sure God looks after you because you are made in His image and were known to Him before you were even born (Jer. 1:5), and that reality is not diminished when you become a teenager!

On this first trip to the USA, the boys were often whisked away for exciting activities and outings by our new friends, who so kindly showed them true Christian love. Those were indeed the kindest of gifts from the Lord's hand, and in His mercy the boys witnessed firsthand love in action. In fact, they still have fond memories of crazy golf; ice cream; visiting parks; and, of course, playing games and eating pizza at Chuck E. Cheese. All of this gave the boys a good idea of what lay ahead for them when we finally made the big move. Emigration was no longer such a scary prospect, but one to be embraced. The children trusted the faith and confidence of their parents and grasped the will of their Father in heaven with a childlike confidence. It also reminded them that, wherever in the world they went, the Lord's people would be there and would love and care for them as brothers in Christ.

However, on our return home from the visit, the enormity of the impending move hit us. The boys were greeted back in Scotland by all that was familiar and that they loved: our home, the village school, our church family, and our friends in the neighborhood. The two worlds were radically different. Our job as parents was to bridge that gap and then to reassure them that moving to America was the Lord's will for us. Despite the upheaval, we remained confident that His ways are not our ways; that our Father in heaven would never leave us or forsake us. These are great truths, and yet there were moments when they were hard to inwardly digest. That is why it is so important to read and to hear God's Word, reminding us of these truths every day. I would exhort you, dear PK, to ground yourself in the Word of God so that when such circumstances come upon you, you can run back to what you know is truth.

There was one moment before the final move when we as parents looked on in amusement. We had asked our boys to go through their toys and decide which ones they could leave behind and to give to our church's "bring and buy" sale (similar to a garage sale). We hoped in this way to rid our house of excess toys and make packing up a little easier. We were dismayed to discover that the boys returned from the church sale with more toys than they had taken to sell!

In God's kind providence during the lead-up to the move, we were amazed to repeatedly hear the radio playing the wonderful song "Sailing to Philadelphia" by Mark Knopfler and James Taylor. It was a hit and seemed to be playing all the time. We would hold the boys' hands and dance to it in our living room, making them more and more excited about emigrating. Of course, this is now just a fun memory, but during that time of transition it proved to be an important way of encouraging the excitement and anticipation that were beginning to build.

Despite all this, the day of the final move remained a hard reality. The boys sadly realized that they would no longer be able to visit grandparents simply by jumping into the car to go to England or hopping on the ferry to visit the Isle of Lewis. Such visits would now take great planning and be very expensive. We as a family had already said our goodbyes to loved ones—sisters, parents, and elderly aunts and uncles. Knowing that we might never see some of our older relatives again was particularly distressing. We reminded ourselves that, whatever happened in the future, we would still see them in heaven. That did not remove the sorrow of parting, but it pointed us forward toward the great hope of the Christian faith, that any suffering in this life is as nothing compared to the great glory that is to come (2 Cor. 4:17–18).

Mercifully, we had professional packers, and as a family we looked on with much anticipation as our precious belongings were carefully packed and loaded. Included were our many china tea sets—precious wedding gifts from great aunts on the Isle of Lewis (who were convinced that I would one day find that my husband was a pastor)—and many, many books on subjects ranging from politics to theology. John and Peter watched in amazement as their bikes were sprayed with disinfectant to avoid transporting any viruses to America! In no time at all our home was empty, all our belongings packed up. And the Lord again interspersed a moment of hilarity; the truck was not big enough—too many books! You're probably all too familiar with that sight! And so, a second container was needed to ship the library. Oh, the joys of moving a pastor to another continent!

Though we can look back and see the funny moments that happened in the process of packing and moving, it was in fact a very sobering experience. Our two sons were overwhelmed with real grief and sadness as we pulled away in the car from our beloved Scottish home. Their friends ran after the car, waving and crying and shouting goodbye, until they could keep up no more and slipped slowly into the distance. As parents, we felt deeply the pain and anguish of our sons. Friends are a precious gift of God, and to be parted from them or to lose them is exceptionally hard. That evening, as we sat in our hotel room at the airport, we held them close, prayed with them, and reassured them that God's plans are always perfect.

Notwithstanding all this, it was still hard to explain to wee boys who had left behind all they had ever known, loved, and cared for that all would work out for God's glory and our blessing. As we said at the start, we never see the full picture of our lives and actions as God does. We see the present moment and little beyond it. That is why faith is so important, because it reminds us of the greater reality of God's love and care, even when we cannot see them immediately. Gospel ministry comes with a high price tag, and often it means such heart wrenching partings.

For a family living in the north of Scotland, traveling to Philadelphia meant catching two planes: from Aberdeen to London and then from

London to Philadelphia. As we took off from Aberdeen and watched the beautiful landscape disappear below the clouds, we knew that we were leaving behind everything that was familiar and embarking on a voyage that would culminate in our family embracing a new way of life, a different cultural mindset, and many new opportunities and challenges. Yet we were reminded in Scripture that God never changes; He is the same yesterday, today, and forever. This truth gave us great comfort at a time when our world was in chaos and we were on our way into the unknown. That way was unknown to us, but not unknown to God. He remains the God who has numbered the very hairs on our heads (Luke 12:7).

Consider with me the beautiful story of Ruth the Moabitess. Her husband died, leaving her with a life that must have seemed very bleak, even hopeless. Yet she left all that she knew and traveled with her beloved mother-in-law, Naomi, to be with the Lord's people, who were now her people. She, too, faced the unknown, yet the Lord reveals to us in His Word that this act of faith and trust was blessed by Him. The Lord's providence in Ruth's life was remarkable. Though humanly speaking there seem to have been a plethora of coincidences in her story, they were all part of God's perfect plan for her life. Ruth was provided with shelter, food, and ultimately the love and care of Boaz, who became her kinsman-redeemer. Adding even greater glory to her story, she became the great grandmother of David, the greatest king of Israel in the Old Testament and one whose life pointed so clearly to the coming of the Lord Jesus Christ as Savior. What a wonderful picture of the Lord's care for His own!

Our two boys always traveled well, and as they gazed out of the plane's window as we flew from London to Philadelphia, their little noses pressed on the glass, we witnessed the delights of our sons gazing out in awe at the beauty and wonder of the world the Lord had made. The hands that flung stars into space and separated light from darkness, created the expanse of the sky and the waters beneath—all of this was made clear to two little boys that day as they gazed down on the earth.

Arriving in Philadelphia, we were greeted by intense heat and humidity, a brutal summer's day in the USA. Everything seemed so far removed from the village life in rural Scotland—life we had left just twenty-four hours before. America seemed bigger, noisier, and more alien, especially to our boys. The slow pace of life they had enjoyed had accelerated to a trot, if not a gallop.

Even the sounds were unfamiliar—birds and insects we did not have in the UK. We remember especially one occasion that summer when our boys were playing in the garden and suddenly stopped, looks of puzzlement on their little faces. They had heard the chirp of a bird they had never come across before and were instinctively intrigued. This moment is forever embedded in my mind as the time when one of God's "American" creatures introduced itself for the first time to two little British boys.

Before long, we took possession of our new home, and as a family we settled into life in the States. Our boys began the new school year. Peter entered first grade with grim determination and John third grade with an air of nervous expectation—different personalities facing these new circumstances in different ways. We had always encouraged our boys to bring their requests before the Lord, so their cares and concerns regarding this new adventure in their lives were brought each night before the throne of grace. The boys were often reminded that the Lord delights to hear the prayers of His little ones and takes joy in His children bringing them to Him.

Those of you who are anxious should always remember the power of prayer. Just as our earthly parents love to talk to us and reassure us, so our heavenly Father delights to hear our prayers and our concerns. As we call out to Him for help and reassurance, so His Spirit will work in our hearts to give us confidence that He does indeed care for us and will guide our steps. Sometimes the way ahead looks dark and scary, but God has promised that He will never leave us and never forsake us, and as we talk to Him we will know that with increasing certainty.

Church, too, was a haven. There the boys were under the preaching of the Word, the gospel was faithfully proclaimed, and voices were lifted in worship to our great God. There was nothing new here! All over the world, the Word is used to convict, instruct, and point to Christ. As in Scotland, our boys were loved by believers who cared for them. The familiar experience of belonging to a church body was a reminder to our precious sons that, though many miles, mountains, and seas separated them from the church family they had left behind, the Lord would provide for them exactly what they needed and desired—the American church family became their church family.

This is one of the greatest blessings of the Christian life. Wherever you go in the world, there are other Christians. Often they look different. Perhaps they have different colored skin. Often they sound different. They may even speak different languages and typically have a radically different culture. But they all have one thing in common binding them together: their love for the Lord Jesus Christ, their Savior. And that means when you move to unknown places and meet other Christians, it is just like meeting new friends or new members of your family. Even though you may have never met previously, you already share the most precious commonality—sins forgiven and hearts filled with the love of God.

That was exactly what we found in America. Yes, the people in church talked with a different accent. They even sang familiar hymns to tunes with which we were not familiar. But when they talked about Jesus, we were unquestionably connected. And it was the same for our boys. They had left precious Christian friends back home, but they found new, like-minded Christian friends in America.

Looking at the providence of God over the years, we have seen His hand gently guiding us, sometimes chastising us, but always pointing to His might, power, and glory, as displayed in His Son, the Lord Jesus Christ. Our two sons have been a delight to us, and as we have witnessed their growth over the years we have seen two young men come to trust in the Lord, grasping by faith all that they have been taught. They have both now left home, studied, graduated from university, and are now forging their own paths in this world. Yes, of course, they have had their struggles, as will you, but we are told in God's Word that our life on earth is not supposed to be easy. However, when we place our confidence and trust in the Rock of our salvation our steps are steadied, and, being grounded in God's Word, we know that the Lord has always been with His children in the past, is so today, and will be in the future.

What a great God we have! Let me remind you again: He is the One who numbers the hairs on our heads and will not let a sparrow fall to the ground without His knowledge. He will carry us when we are weary and heavy laden. So, pastors' children, if you are anxious about the possibility of moving or have moved and are in a strange and unfamiliar land or city, remember that the Lord tells us that we are not to be anxious about what we will eat or drink or what clothing we will wear. The Bible tells us that God knows we need these things. And He will provide for those needs in accordance with His perfect will (Matt. 6:25, 32–33).

As we end our letter, there is one beautiful Christian saying that has given us and our boys great comfort over the years, especially at times of great challenge or change. It is the first question and answer of the Heidelberg Catechism, a wonderful statement of the Christian faith written by godly men centuries ago but that still holds true today. It reads as follows:

> What is your only comfort in life and death?
>
> That I am not my own, but belong with body and soul, both in life and in death, to my faithful Savior Jesus Christ. He has fully paid for all my sins with his precious blood, and has set me free from all the power of the devil. He also preserves me in such a way that without the will of my heavenly Father not a hair can fall from my head; indeed, all things must work together for my salvation. Therefore, by his Holy Spirit he also assures me of eternal life and makes me heartily willing and ready from now on to live for him.

These words are true. There are innumerable circumstances in life that can worry or disturb us. Emigration to another country is only one of them. The answer to them all is Jesus Christ. He is our comfort. And we must remember to keep our focus on Him, both in prayer and whenever circumstances leave us frightened or confused.

We hope that our story has been of help to you, and we wish you God's blessing—and indeed His comfort.

With love,
Carl and Catriona Trueman

Carl and Catriona have been married for thirty years and currently live in Slippery Rock in Western Pennsylvania. They have two wonderful sons, John (twenty-seven) and Peter (twenty-five). Catriona is originally from the Isle of Lewis, and Carl was born in Birmingham, England, but was raised in the Cotswolds.

DEPRESSION
The Dark Night of the Soul

Neil and Catherine Stewart

Let me start by saying that growing up in a pastor's home has many benefits. We are deeply immersed in Christianity and the church in a way that most children do not get to experience. If your home is anything like mine, your father probably leads family worship; your mother is involved in many undefined roles, in multiple ways around the church; and you and your siblings seem to be there every time the doors are open. All of this can have numerous blessings on your soul. I say "can" because if you're anything like me, then you can also become numb to the blessings you get to encounter on a daily basis. This "numbness" presents quite subtly at times—a coldness of heart, depression, rebellion, or an undetected passive aggressive manner—and yet you must remind yourself that the cocoon of ministry does not automatically grant you immunity from straying from Christ.

While a struggle with depression is not one that I have personally had to work through, I have struggled with loneliness. Of course, these are remarkably different challenges, and yet they both have the potential to bring significant pain and sorrow into our lives. My parents have been a constant in my life, and this remains incredible to me as I ponder what that has entailed. They have sat up late at night with me during many hard times. They repeatedly pointed me to Christ when my heart was not focused on Him. They have been a safe place to cry in the darkest of days, but, most importantly, they (with the help of God) have given the best advice I could have asked for throughout my earthly life. They have had their hands full with me, and I know that they have counseled many other people through many other situations. I could not imagine a couple more equipped to write this letter. Read slowly, digest, and put into practice all that they recommend. I promise you won't regret learning from them.

Your fellow PK,

Hannah

Dear Pastor's Kid,

The burden of depression is common in ministry families, and it is not one to be borne alone. Isolation is the predator's strategy, and Satan loves to separate the weak from the flock and then move in for the kill. This tactic is particularly effective when the church itself is the most obvious cause of our sense of pain, loneliness, and betrayal. We face the temptation to draw back, to erect walls, to bar-up the windows of our souls—like houses in the rough end of town. The safety we feel inside, however, is illusory and suffocating. Trying to keep dangerous people out, we trap ourselves in. Safe from threats, yes, but also trapped away from the one community God designed to help us, the church. For all her faults, she remains God's appointed answer to our longing for a safe place, a harbor amidst the storms of life, a healing community in which our souls can thrive.

With this in mind, I want to encourage you, when the darkness closes in, to lean into the church. Ask your parents to find a community of peers and mentors you can trust within her walls. Sometimes this might necessitate connecting to a local sister congregation. But one thing remains certain: God is always to be found first and best under the preaching of His Word, amid His people. You will need both His help and this community to lead you through the sticky labyrinth of depression—what our fathers used to call "the dark night of the soul."

Another challenge we must face up front is the stigma that often surrounds depression. Christians usually feel embarrassed, and perhaps even a little bit ashamed, to admit such dark feelings. Ours is a religion of joy, we think, so Christians aren't "supposed" to get depressed! Please hear me when I say this: *nothing could be further from the truth*!

To be sure, in the beginning, before man fell into sin, depression had no part in God's creation. But now, in the east-of-Eden world we inherit, with souls scarred by our first father's wretched choice, we should expect sadness, shame, and darkness to be frequent companions.

At times, it will seem as though everything is against us and all hope is lost. But as is so very often the case, the appearance of things and their reality are quite different. Our feelings are seldom to be trusted; faith must reach through topsy-turvy emotional instability and lay hold of the surer foundation lying always beneath the Christian.

The Psalms

To help us through such seasons, God has given us the Psalter.

Calvin called this sacred songbook the anatomy of the Christian soul; it shows us how the Christian life is supposed to feel. With sixty-two laments in the collection, God seems to know that our feelings will often be very far from upbeat. How could they not be?

The psalmist often faced insurmountable odds (Ps. 3:1–3), expressed a depressing litany of personal failure (Psalms 32 and 51), perceived the foundations collapsing all around him (Ps. 11:3), and experienced a God who at best seemed to be hiding (Psalm 13) or who at worst seems against him altogether (Psalms 6 and 38).

In such a world, joy is often surprising in its appearance, and always supernatural in its source. Take Psalm 46, for example: Everything is coming unglued. Even the mountains—those ever-constant, always standing, immoveable reference points of life, are depicted as falling into the midst of the sea (vv. 1–3). Then the camera angle pans in on Mount Zion (remember what is happening to the mountains!). You would expect to find panic here, but instead there is joy—counter-predictable gladness in the life-giving presence of God, flowing like a river through His dwelling place (Ps. 46:4 and the verses following).

God gives us such songs beforehand. They shine like beacons in the night, pointing us home to God. They teach the secret of spiritual sanity: whatever life throws your way, we face life best by facing God first, with a song in our souls. They also point inward, helping us understand the pain we feel so keenly.

They whisper reassuringly: see, others have felt this way before. You are not alone. You have a brother in the psalmist, one made of the same stuff you are, someone who understands your pain from the inside. Your heart is not malfunctioning; life is supposed to feel this way east of Eden.

When the world inside and outside spins like a roulette wheel, these songs form a reference point of experiential theology, a quiet place to shelter amidst the storm, a sanctuary of rest where the weary soul can meet God, a golden thread leading through the inexorable labyrinth of life in a fallen world.

Most of the time, these songs leave the psalmist better than they found him. But not always. In Psalm 88, for example, which Alec Motyer calls "one of the most moving psalms in the whole collection," we find a song

> without any note of hope, the product of a time of apparently terminal and prolonged illness, and, appropriately to its mood throughout, it ends with the bleak word "darkness" in verse 18. The three sections of the psalm each beginning with a renewed appeal to the Lord (1–9a, 9b–12, 13–18), deal in turn with life without comfort, death without hope, and questions without answers. But prayer is still the way when all hope is gone: the sufferer in all his darkness is still the intercessor.

In other words, no matter how dark things seem, no matter how discouraged we become, the Christian response must never be to draw back from God. We find our bearings through the darkness leaning in to Him.

Why Do Christians Become Depressed?

I know you feel quite sure your depression finds its origin in sin—your sins of commission and omission, as well as the sins of others and your own sinful response to them. This is at least part, or perhaps even most, of the story. But in my experience, the streams of pain feeding into a person's depression are usually legion. Together, they form a tangled web of physical, psychological, and spiritual barbed wire. So, a broad approach will serve us best here.

We Are Enfleshed Souls

When I counsel someone struggling with depression, I always make sure to ask about their physical health. Some Christians tend to neglect this side of a person's story, preferring to see depression as purely and simply a failure of faith, or as a refusal to obey the command to "Rejoice always, and again I say rejoice!" Such an approach is one-sided and naïve. We must not ignore the physicality of our frames, and the union they enjoy (or endure) with our souls. Chronic pain, infection, inflammation, hormonal imbalances, gastrointestinal upset, arthritis, migraine headaches, and myriad other continuing or acute conditions can all take their toll, deplete our energy, and leave us in the grip of daily malaise (feeling crummy). So, I would encourage you to enlist the help of a competent physician to assess your background level of health.

Other factors to consider include the following.

Sleep

What time do you normally retire in the evening, and when do you normally rise in the morning? How well do you sleep during the night?

Do you commonly find yourself waking early in the morning, unable to get back to sleep? This can be a sign of what doctors call "clinical depression." When you wake in the morning, do you feel rested? Does anyone in your family struggle with sleep apnea? If you are known to snore, have you ever visited a doctor to evaluate your breathing during sleep?

Diet

Do you eat a healthy, balanced diet? Are you at a normal weight? Being under- and overweight can very much affect the way we feel.

Exercise

Are you physically fit? Do you get enough exercise each week?

Physical activity is a natural antidepressant associated with the release of endorphins (natural, morphine-like chemicals that reduce pain and induce a sense of well-being). If you are not physically fit, I would encourage you to get a checkup with your doctor to see if you are well enough to start an exercise program, and perhaps get some advice as to how you might do so.

Hormones

Have you had your various hormone levels checked recently (for example, the hormones produced by the thyroid gland play an important part in our ability to think clearly and quickly, our sense of motivation, and our mood)?

Productivity

It is normal for people who feel depressed to report that they feel stuck in the mud, that they are thinking their way through mental treacle and just can't seem to get things done.

In such cases, depression is clearly the cause of their lack of productivity. For others, however, the reverse is the case. I would be interested to hear about your work habits before you became depressed. Were you productive then? Were you getting the right things done, at the right time, in the right way, and to the right end? In our increasingly distracted age, I frequently see young people who are frankly addicted to video games (typically more of a male problem), social media, and pornography. Such habitual unproductivity tends to leave us feeling as though we are failing at life. Live this way for long, and it will certainly take its toll on your soul.

Drugs

What medications are you on? If you are taking long-term medications prescribed by more than one physician, it is always a good idea to have a doctor look at the list. Some medications, either by themselves or in combination with other drugs, are known to cause depressive symptoms. It is also important to be honest regarding any illicit use of alcohol or other "recreational" drugs.

You should also consider your caffeine intake. I have seen a number of young people suffering symptoms of insomnia and chronic anxiety stemming from the overconsumption of energy drinks. If this is the case, slowly wean yourself off them over the course of several weeks and see how that helps things.

Family History

In some families, a proneness to depression can run through the generations. This may point to a genetic/familial tendency toward melancholy. If such cases, when the darkness does not lift over the course of a few weeks, I would encourage you to seek medical help for your depression (I'll get to that at the end of this letter).

Times Are Hard

Our circumstances can open the door to depression. Job was right when he observed that "man is born to trouble, as the sparks fly upward" (Job 5:7). From bacteria to bull sharks and from viruses to vipers, there is a sharp edge to the created order that threatens pain at every turn.

Responding to this with anger; bitterness; resentment; and, above all, unbelief never serves us well. Such a reaction always betrays a soul that has lost sight of God and His fatherly hand of providence.

We need grace for the willingness to pray, as expressed by Jerry Bridges, "Lord, I am willing to receive what you give, to lack what you withhold, to relinquish what you take, and to be what you require."

All You Need Is Love

It is not only life that can be much harder than it ought to be; relationships can, too—especially those with our nearest and dearest ones. These relationships can also seed some of our darkest emotions. An aggressive selfishness grips the children of men. Those who are hostile toward God will not often be friendly toward one another.

So very often, back behind our darkest human experiences lies the longing for love. Billy Joel summed it up well:

> You just need one—one person out of millions—to know and accept and love you for being, well, just the way you are.... I see old folks walking down the street who look like they've been together 50 years, and there's something very touching about it—that they've lasted so long. I used to wonder: How come I don't have that? I can dream about it, think about it, write music and lyrics and sing about it. I can even try to achieve it again, and often have.... You can have all the money in the world, you can have mansions, you can have properties, you can have yachts, you can have limousines, you can have motorcycles, but without love, "it doesn't mean a...thing."

When the Church Is Not a Refuge

Children of the manse are particularly vulnerable here. When the parents of other children struggle at work, it's difficult, but they can at least turn to the church for help. For them, the body of Christ is one of God's great antidotes to the stressors of life. But when the pastor falls out with the church (or a faction therein), not only are the children deprived of this refuge, but for them the haven can become a hell hole.

I have heard pastors' kids describe the following stressors:

- The pain of watching many of their father's friends—people he loved, served, into whom he poured his very soul—turn against him.

- The sense of dread each Sunday, knowing people are talking about their dad, complaining about him, and viewing his words and deeds in the worst possible light.

- The loneliness and alienation they feel in the face of cold, dead-fish handshakes, paper-thin smiles, and veneered niceness.

- Feeling like a leper in the youth group, always the outsider, excluded from the cool-kid cliques.

- The bitter discontentment of watching their parents struggle to get by on meager means, hearing how the deacons refuse to give their dad a cost of living raise each year (because they reward performance, not the passing of a year), all of which leaves their mom trying to spread less and less butter over more and more bread.

- The snide jealousy of some in the church who feel their dad makes "far too much money."

- The church gossip who remarked at the door, "I love your new car. I wish my husband could afford a car like that!" Then there was the time one pastor let slip that the reason for their "staycation" last year was that they couldn't afford to go away, and how the deacon responded, "Ah, but your reward is in heaven!" Ouch!

- The time the church fired one PK's dad and suddenly they lost all their friends, their town, their school, their home, their everything. It was hard not to weep as they described driving out of town for the last time into the great unknown. Where would they go next? What would become of them?

When the church fails you, try to remember the following things.

Don't Forget the Devil
First, the devil is always active, causing trouble in the church. Forgetting this only compounds our pain. Remember when, in Matthew 16, Peter tried to discourage our brave Savior from going to the cross and Jesus rightly perceived that this thought didn't originate in the mind of His friend. "Get behind Me, Satan!" (v. 23), he said to His friend. Never forget: the church might be God's sheep, but we are all silly sheep at best, too prone to listen to the devil. Sin clouds our best judgments, confuses our best thoughts, corrupts our best desires, and confounds our best efforts. We are all hurting sheep, prone to hurt others and easily hurt by them!

Here Be Dragons
It's also good to remember that not all in the church are sheep. If we liken the body of Christ to a map, we will find many regions marked "Here be dragons and wolves!"

What a Friend We Have in Jesus
In all of this, the wise Christian will take care to connect all their sorrows to the Lord. He is always the first cause of every pang of sorrow we feel, for He is also the sovereign Lord over all our trials.

You might think this knowledge would make your depression worse. But actually, this truth is often the only pathway to hope, sanity, and true worship. Again, the psalmist helps us:

Oh, bless our God, you peoples!
And make the voice of His praise to be heard,
Who keeps our soul among the living,
And does not allow our feet to be moved.

For You, O God, have tested us;
You have refined us as silver is refined.
You brought us into the net;
You laid affliction on our backs.

You have caused men to ride over our heads;
We went through fire and through water;
But You brought us out to rich fulfillment. (Ps. 66:8–12)

108 SURVIVING THE FISHBOWL

Check Your Conclusions

Our interpretation of difficult situations (and of difficult people) can also feed into this toxic mix.

By our very nature, human beings are meaning makers. We can't help ourselves. We connect the dots (or try to) in an effort to make sense out of life. We like to know what happened and why. We also like to predict what might happen next.

These assessments are never 100 percent accurate. Think of Abraham's depressing conclusion regarding his likely life expectancy, given his wife's beauty amidst the godless men of Egypt (Gen. 12:11–12). Or think of Sarai's assessment of her own fertility status, and what action they, as a couple, needed to take next in order to start a family (Gen. 16:2). Lot's daughters were similarly unhelpful in evaluating their marriage prospects (Gen. 19:31 and the verses following). We could also speak of Esau, in a moment of ravenous hunger weighing up the comparative value of a cup of soup against his birthright (Genesis 36), Moses's negative self-assessment as a potential prophet (Ex. 4:10), Israel's dismay at the lack of 7-Elevens in the wilderness (Exodus 17 is one example), or David's risk assessment regarding his chances of prevailing in his battle against Saul (1 Sam. 27:1).

The list of biblical examples goes on and on.

Usually, the trouble with such reasoning is that we forget to factor God into the equation of life. Make this mistake, and our reasoning will sound much more like the first half of Psalm 11 than the second.

In the LORD I put my trust;
How can you say to my soul,
"Flee as a bird to your mountain"?
For look! The wicked bend their bow,
They make ready their arrow on the string,
That they may shoot secretly at the upright in heart.
If the foundations are destroyed,
What can the righteous do? (Ps. 11:1–3)

This is the voice of doubt, of unbelief, of despair; and notice that, beyond that opening verse, it says nothing of God and suggests nothing but the

dereliction of faith. David's response is salutary, reminding himself of
God and his duty to trust Him.

> The LORD is in His holy temple,
> The LORD's throne is in heaven;
> His eyes behold,
> His eyelids test the sons of men.
> The LORD tests the righteous,
> But the wicked and the one who loves violence His soul hates.
> Upon the wicked He will rain coals;
> Fire and brimstone and a burning wind
> Shall be the portion of their cup.
>
> For the LORD is righteous,
> He loves righteousness;
> His countenance beholds the upright. (Ps. 11:4–7)

Sliding down into the pit of despair, David finds stays for his hands and
feet: God's throne, God's eye, and God's character. Like grass seed sown
in the fall's warm, moist soil, ideas of hope germinate left and right:
somewhere, somehow, someone is in control of this mess. His throne,
in the temple where sacrifices are made and received, is friendly to sinners. I am not lost in the crowd; God lives and sees me. He will not let
evil have the last word. My best days lie yet ahead.

What a difference good theology makes in tight places!

What about those days when God seems to be against us, when we
sense He is the first cause of all our pain? How are we to respond when
God feels vicious and vindictive? Ask Jeremiah. He was not called the
weeping prophet for nothing.

> I am the man who has seen affliction by the rod of His wrath.
> He has led me and made me walk
> In darkness and not in light.
> Surely He has turned His hand against me
> Time and time again throughout the day.
>
> He has aged my flesh and my skin,
> And broken my bones.
> He has besieged me

And surrounded me with bitterness and woe.
He has set me in dark places
Like the dead of long ago.

He has hedged me in so that I cannot get out;
He has made my chain heavy.
Even when I cry and shout,
He shuts out my prayer.
He has blocked my ways with hewn stone;
He has made my paths crooked.

He has been to me a bear lying in wait,
Like a lion in ambush.
He has turned aside my ways and torn me in pieces;
He has made me desolate.
He has bent His bow
And set me up as a target for the arrow.

He has caused the arrows of His quiver
To pierce my loins.
I have become the ridicule of all my people—
Their taunting song all the day.
He has filled me with bitterness,
He has made me drink wormwood.

He has also broken my teeth with gravel,
And covered me with ashes.
You have moved my soul far from peace;
I have forgotten prosperity.
And I said, "My strength and my hope
Have perished from the Lord." (Lam. 3:1–18)

Again, faith—and what faith it took!—reached through the labyrinth,
through the appearance of things and laid hold of a deeper, truer logic:

Remember my affliction and roaming,
The wormwood and the gall.
My soul still remembers
And sinks within me.
This I recall to my mind,
Therefore I have hope.

Through the LORD's mercies we are not consumed,
Because His compassions fail not.
They are new every morning;
Great is Your faithfulness.
"The LORD is my portion," says my soul,
"Therefore I hope in Him!" (Lam. 3:19–24)

In our spiritual battles, we do well to remember that the first piece of spiritual armor is the belt of truth (Eph. 6:14). We have to ground ourselves in what's true—true about God, true about the world, true about ourselves, true about life. If we don't begin here, we will have no firm footing on which to stand.

Our Emotions Scream, but Our Thoughts Whisper

There is almost always a logic to our emotional turmoil that simmers beneath the surface. If you liken an unhelpful emotion to a weed growing in the soul, pull it up and you will find thoughts feeding its roots! Like the background music in a supermarket, these thoughts whisper, almost subliminally, in the background. Most of the time we aren't even aware of their presence.

Think, for example, of a soul overcome with anxiety. Perhaps you can remember a time when you felt that way. You feel anxiety like a rubber band doubled (or tripled) across your shoulders, up and down your spine, and around your temples, like a ravenous rat gnawing out your stomach.

Where does this feeling come from? Usually from your thoughts. Back behind those feelings, your brain is alive with Grima Worm tongue-like whisperings. "What if this happens?" "What if that happens?" "Don't you know Sara is talking about you all up and down the college cafeteria?" "Nobody likes you!" "You'll never amount to anything!" "You failed in this thing just like you fail in everything."

Such thoughts take their toll. Over a lifetime they become habits, shaping the inner dialogue of our soul, like lenses that color the way we see everything. Just like any habit, we begin by making them, and then they return the favor by making us.

As we shall see in a moment, such thoughts do not tell the whole story of depression, but they do form a massive part of it. I don't think I ever met a "clinically" depressed or anxious person who had healthy habits of thought.

Much in the same way professional athletes program muscle memory into their brains, I feel convinced that human beings train their minds to respond to life (good times and bad) with certain patterns of thought.

Imagine your brain as a virgin wheat field. On one side of the wheat field there is a school, and on the other there is a group of children who want to get across the field to learn their day's lessons. What do they do? Well, they make a path through the field. The next day they come back to the field and repeat the process. However, on day two the wheat isn't exactly the same as it was the previous day. Now they can see stalks of wheat that are ever so slightly bent where they walked the day before. I imagine them going that same way again. So, the process continues throughout the term, until the wheat is not just bent along this pathway but trampled all the way to the ground, and then out of existence altogether, as a clear path forms across the field.

In this example, the wheat field represents the neuronal pathways in our brain, and the almost limitless number of potential routes the electrical energy can take as it flows from one side to the other. But over time, because of repeated patterns of thought or action, pathways form—neuronal pathways. Once established, the electrical energy tends to flow this way, whether we want it to or not.

Recognizing this undergirds the importance of Paul's counsel to the Philippians, below, does it not?

> Finally, brethren, whatever things are true, whatever things are noble, whatever things are just, whatever things are pure, whatever things are lovely, whatever things are of good report, if there is any virtue and if there is anything praiseworthy—meditate on these things. (Phil. 4:8)

If we want to feel a way we have never felt before, we must learn to think in a way we have never thought before.

I am indebted to Lou Priolo and his work on "Heart Journals" for this line of thought. Write down your thoughts and record how you respond to the events of life. Put your inner dialogue down on paper. Uncover the thoughts behind all your feelings (good and bad, positive and negative).

Then, with thoughts clearly identified, ask yourself: "What does the Bible say about these thoughts?" "How should I be thinking?" Does God's Word contain truth that speaks into this situation: a promise to believe, a command to obey, an example to follow? With Augustine, pray these truths into your soul: "Give what Thou commandest, and command what Thou willest."

The Voice of God in the Soul of a Man

Feeding into all this, you also have the conscience, what the Puritans called "the voice of God in the soul of a man." In his excellent book *A Quest for Godliness: The Puritan Vision of the Christian Life*, James (J. I.) Packer summed up the Puritan view of the conscience like this: "Conscience, to them, signified a man's knowledge of himself as standing in God's presence (coram Deo, in Luther's phrase), subject to God's word and exposed to the judgement of God's law, and yet—if a believer—justified and accepted nonetheless through divine grace."

The conscience, therefore, tells us whether we are in the right with God or in the wrong with Him. And while it is neither safe nor sound practice to ignore the conscience, it, too, is touched by the fall and cannot always be trusted to lead us either in truth or to God.

Think of the conscience like a sundial. Sundials are designed to tell the time in a specific location under the light of the sun. Move them to a different part of the globe or attempt to read them by the light of the moon (or worse still, by the arbitrary light of a shifting, flashing light) and you will quickly find yourself confused.

So it is with the conscience when it is illumined by any other standard than the law of our God and the gospel of His ever blessed Son. Like anxiety, an offended conscience gnaws at the soul like a ravenous rat.

If we are to maintain equilibrium within, we need to become well versed in dealing with our conscience. When our conscience is offended, we need skill to root the general feeling of "offense" in the particularities of the law (we need to know whether our conscience is right to be bothered, and about what and why).

In that regard, how is your conscience doing? Guard against neurotic introspection here. If there is some life sin causing your depression, you likely already know it. It'll stand out like a cockroach on a cream cake.

You all need to be skillful in applying the gospel to a wounded conscience. Only the gospel can sprinkle away the feeling of uncleanness lingering deep within each human heart (Heb. 10:22). Only the gospel can silence the alarm by saying, "I am no longer liable to the judgment due to this sin. I have given it to Christ, and through His union with me this sin (and the judgment it deserves) has become His very own" (see 2 Cor. 5:21).

Don't Just Sit There: Talk to Yourself

Sometimes our feelings of discouragement are inexplicable. We feel down and don't know why. As always, the psalmist is a friend here, too.

> Why are you cast down, O my soul?
> And why are you disquieted within me?
> Hope in God, for I shall yet praise Him
> For the help of His countenance. (Ps. 42:5)

I love Martyn Lloyd-Jones's famous comment on this verse: "Our problem is that we listen to ourselves too much, when what we really need to be doing is talking to ourselves." Listening to negative thoughts is a passive and a paralyzing habit. Instead, we must develop the active discipline of speaking to ourselves words of faith, hope, and love!

Should Christians Take Antidepressants?

This is an important question, and there is much confusion on this subject in the church. Let's start with some undeniable principles:

- Human beings are enfleshed souls. The physical and chemical nature of our brains provides a way for our souls to interface and interact with the world around us.

- A host of factors can affect the brain's chemical balance.
  Take nicotine receptors, for example. When you expose a brain to nicotine regularly, it produces more nicotine receptors. As a result, the tobacco user becomes tolerant of the effects of nicotine

and experiences symptoms of withdrawal when Nicotine levels drop in their system. These symptoms are not pleasant. One of the reasons people smoke is to keep these unpleasant feelings at bay.

The fall of man compounds all this. The curse of God upon this world affects our bodies, not just our souls. As a result, our body's ability to regulate our blood pressure, glucose levels, electrolyte balances, hormones, etc., is to a greater or lesser extent broken.

- Through the use of medicine and other therapies, God has given man the ability to counteract and alleviate some of this "brokenness." There is clear evidence that antidepressants have a positive effect on many patients suffering from depression.

To be sure, these medicines can themselves have unintended consequences. Doctors must exercise care lest they make things worse, not better. The Hypocratic Oath's "Primum Non Nocere" vow assumes this ("First do no harm"). More study needs to be done on the long-term effects of antidepressants and other psychotropic medicines (for example, some ADHD medications), especially on the adolescent brain. For this reason, in my own family I tend to work on this principle: the younger the child, the more reticent I am to encourage the use of antidepressant (or other psychotropic) medication. I certainly would never encourage their use absent the advice of at least one (and probably two) trustworthy pediatric psychiatrists. We know, for example, that some antidepressants (members of the SSRI class of drugs—selective serotonin reuptake inhibitors) are associated with impulsive behavior and even suicidal thoughts.

- It is *never* safe to stop medicines prescribed by a doctor without medical supervision. This is especially true of antidepressants. Normally, we must be extremely careful to wean ourselves off these medicines. This can take weeks or even months. Stopping them abruptly can have disastrous consequences. *Never* do this without a competent physician's supervision.

- If your depression is severe, lasts more than a few weeks or months, is deepening quickly, and especially if it is associated with suicidal thoughts, then I would strongly encourage you to seek the help of your family physician. You should not feel embarrassed or guilty about taking antidepressant medication.

- Depression can feed on itself, forming a downward death spiral of discouragement. I have heard many Christians testify to how a short-term prescription of antidepressants gave them a leg up out of this spiral, helping them get their thoughts moving again in a helpful direction. David Murray's excellent little book *Christians Get Depressed Too* provides a helpful description of this effect.

  Some Christians—even godly, earnest Christians who trust God wholeheartedly—find that they need the help of antidepressants on a more long-term basis. I can think of at least one man, whom I regard as a tremendous example of godliness in action, who has testified to me on numerous occasions, "Pastor, I take a low dose antidepressant every day. It keeps me on an even keel. I find if I stop taking them, a darkness slowly begins to overwhelm me." This in no way diminishes my respect for this brother. This prescription is as basic to his health as blood pressure medication, lipid lowering drugs, or antibiotics.

- Faith is always the answer for our soul's walk with God, but it is not always the only answer for our body's walk through illness and pain.

Well, there you have it. This letter was a good deal longer than I had planned. I cannot imagine that anything I have said has done the trick to "fix" your struggle. There are no easy answers for our complex souls. But I do hope this letter forms a framework for you to work through. Echoing the gist of Tolkein's famous words at the start of *The Hobbit*, while these words might not mark the beginning of the end of your depression, I pray they just might mark the end of its beginning.

Press on,

Neil and Catherine Stewart

Neil, Catherine, their six children, and Mr. Baxter (their intrepid Rat Terrier) live in Greensboro, North Carolina, where Neil pastors Christ Covenant Church (ARP). Catherine has also written *Letters to Pastor's Wives: When Seminary Ends and Ministry Begins* (P&R). Before moving to America in 1999, Neil worked as a pediatrician at the Royal Belfast Hospital for Sick Children. He has also pastored churches in rural Mississippi and Savannah, Georgia.

REBEL PK
The One Who Got Away (Almost)

Ike Reeder

Almost everyone knows this designation as shorthand for preacher's or pastor's kid! Perhaps you grew up in a church and heard someone say, "well... you know, he's a PK," followed by a knowing glance and then the inevitable words—"Oh yeah, a preacher's kid!" The fact is, it is hard to imagine the pressure that the children who grow up in the home of a pastor must feel and experience as they live their life in the church. The multifaceted pressures, temptations, and challenges are varied and incessant. Everyone, particularly in the church, feels the liberty to comment not only on the pastor's life, but also on his marriage, his family, and his children. Imagine the life of the PK, being asked questions regularly and unabashedly by adults, such as—"What really goes on in your home?" or "Do your parents ever argue with each other?" or "What is your dad really like at home?" or "How does your father discipline you?" In addition, there is another pitfall for the PK. This pitfall is the temptation, because of all the attention received, to feel special or elevated. On top of all that, there is the challenge of feeling a deep-seated resentment that you are constantly being evaluated by others, the pressure to meet the expectation of others. While I am sure that all of the above regularly and sometimes intensely faced all three of the children in our family, we were also blessed to watch each of them uniquely navigate the journey of adolescence as a PK.

Now you have the privilege in the following chapter to read an interesting, informative, and honest communication from one of our children. He was the middle child (which has its own challenges!) and is my only son and namesake—only serving to heighten those challenges!

Cindy and I were blessed by all three of our children, and it is a source of abounding joy to see them personally confess and follow Christ as adults, while they now raise their children in and for the Lord.

I do have a confession. When my son gave me the chapter you are about to read, there was much in it that I knew and some things I didn't know (which were both interesting and at times surprising!). I have personally found his insights instructive, and my guess is that you will also. I am absolutely sure this chapter will not only be a page turner but significantly encouraging, likely surprising, and certainly insightful—so read on!

Warmly,
Harry Reeder, senior pastor,
Briarwood Presbyterian Church

Dear Pastor's Kid,

Though we are separated by time, distance, years, and words on the page, I feel that our shared experiences forge a unique bond of camaraderie and unity shared by relatively few in this world. I, too, have been subject to the unending gaze of the multitude. I, too, know what it's like to bear the weight of expectations. I, too, have felt the added pressures of relationships and responsibility that come with living life in the fishbowl.

I may be dating myself a little bit here, but I remember when I was a teenager and I first heard the song "Limelight" by the Canadian band Rush. You may know them from their classic tune "Tom Sawyer," and, to be sure, that song has many potential overlaps with the life of a pastor's kid. But "Limelight" was the song that always stuck with me. Indeed, there are several similarities between growing up as a PK and being a rock star, as some have noted before.

> Cast in this unlikely role
> Ill-equipped to act
> With insufficient tact
> One must put up barriers
> To keep oneself intact…
> —Rush, "Limelight" © 1981

Wow. Those words totally captured for me what it felt like to grow up in the home of an exceptionally gifted pastor, in a growing church, where responsibility was shared like it was candy. "Ill-equipped to act" for an "unlikely role," I felt as though I were constantly putting "up barriers" just to "keep oneself intact."

I bet you feel like that sometimes, too, don't you? Does the "fish-eye lens" of the crowd, the congregation, feel like it catches you sometimes…or at least most of the time? How many times have you heard, "Hey, Johnny, there's a new boy in the church. Why don't you go over there and make him feel welcome?"

"I have no heart to lie. I can't pretend a stranger is a long-awaited friend."

Before I go on with my letter to you, let me tell you a couple of things to start off with. First, I deeply love my family. I love my father and my mother and my two sisters. I was a middle child, the "peacemaker" of the three. Now I worship and serve in the same church where my father preaches and leads, raising my own family there. I am now forty-five years old and have had a long time to contemplate those (seemingly) tumultuous years of growing up in a pastor's family. I am well removed from the existential trauma of my youth, and even removed from the self-imposed existential trauma of my twenties and thirties.

In fact, the hardest thing about writing this letter to you has been digging back into the past and the emotions, doubts, and sincere feelings that I probably haven't confronted or examined for years and years. Writing this chapter has been cathartic and instructive for me—as a leader, seminary president, network builder, husband, and stepfather (yes, you read that right; I'm the stepfather to two amazing kids—more on that later). I won't pretend that I can step right back into the shoes of the young man—teenager, really—who would get into his car and drive four hours from Charlotte to the beach, step out of the car, walk out into the ocean, stand there for thirty minutes, then get back into the car and drive back to Charlotte. All so I could feel like I was able to get away from it all.

So yes, I rebelled. I did not rebel as hard as some; I rebelled harder and longer than others. As you grow older, my young friend, you will find others who push boundaries harder. You will find still others who don't seem to push boundaries at all. And you will wonder at both while you find out that God draws each of us to Him in His own special way, but always through the only Way—Jesus Christ.

In fact, I am much more interested in the story of how God has the mercy needed to pull someone like myself into a relationship of love and grace than I am in my own story. Because I've learned that I don't want God to be part of my story—I want to be part of His story.

I was on a trip recently with several pastor friends, and one of them was sharing some of the questions that a young Muslim woman who had been visiting his church was asking of him. He loved it. She asked the best questions! One question she asked was this: "How can a God who is defined by His holiness and who is truly omnipresent not simply eradicate the entirety of human existence because of its sin?" What a great question! We often ask the question, "Why is sin such a big deal?" We think about it from our human perspective. She was learning to see our sin from God's perspective. The biggest idol in my life as a kid was the desperate desire to know that my life had significance. The biggest lesson I learned when I finally bowed the knee to my Lord and Savior was that my life has significance only in Christ. And what significance it is! I'm an adopted son of God! I'm an heir to the throne of heaven! My own feeble attempts at significance paled in comparison.

So, in this letter, I am going to cover a few things. First, I am going to tell you how I went from being a young man who hated the responsibilities of being in the "royal family" of a pastor to running a seminary that trains pastors. I am going to leave out a lot of the more sordid details because they simply aren't worth dwelling on. The "fun" of sin is long gone, and only the consequences remain. Second, I am going to briefly write to you about two types of rebellion and ask you to consider some thoughts about them both. Third, I am going to make a few points about the church and hurting people and where you, as a pastor's kid, fit into that mix. Finally, I am going to wrap up my letter to you by giving you three pieces of counsel.

One last note: I'm pretty sure that if someone had handed me this book when I was going into high school or heading off to college, it would have ended up somewhere in the heap of unread gifted books in the back of my closet, or possibly stuck on one of my bookshelves, nicely displayed but with an unbroken spine. I imagine there will be a goodly number of pastors and pastors' wives who pick up this book and read it, trying to get some insight into their families, their children, and the future. Or maybe they're trying to get some ideas about how to deal with a son or daughter who is already in clear rebellion against the Spirit and how they have tried to raise them up. Pastor, pastor's wife—if that is you reading this right now, then stay with me. I think there is much here for you, too.

The Perfect Family

Appearances can sometimes be pretty deceiving. We've all heard that phrase before, right? On a cold February day in 1983, when Harry Reeder showed up in Charlotte with his young family, it looked like just another pastor and his crew beginning a new church plant. And in a sense, it was. There were no hidden sins, no trauma lurking under the surface, and the kids became relatively well adjusted to their new home. The appearance certainly was positive. There were no significant marital problems between Harry and Cindy, and, for the most part, the three children—Jennifer (eleven), Ike (seven), and Abigail (six)—got along well with each other.

Fast-forward thirty-seven years, and the year is 2020. The entire family now lives in Birmingham, not Charlotte. Jennifer went through a premarital pregnancy and moved to Alaska to marry the child's father. She had two more children and eventually went through a divorce. She is now married to another PK, and they have a blended family with five children.

That cute, grinning boy in Charlotte in 1983? Yep, that was me. He would go on to walk completely away from his faith by the time he was nineteen years old; become a Christian when he was twenty-one, after having experienced two years of depression and a destructive lifestyle; repeat that cycle; find his footing in the Lord after a life-threatening illness in his early thirties; and, at the age of thirty-eight, eventually meet a wonderful woman, Angie. At the age of thirty-nine, he married Angie and inherited two wonderful stepchildren.

The youngest daughter, Abigail, would stand firm in her faith, get married at twenty-two, have three children, and become a successful interior designer, working full-time while still being a remarkable mother.

So, what happened? Were Harry and Cindy good parents for one kid and not good parents for another? Was the fallout of poor choices the kids' fault for not trusting in Jesus? How did this family go from being the "picture-perfect family" to a family that has experienced God's grace through difficult circumstances, through rejection of faith?

I can tell you only that I know two things are true: that faithful are the wounds of a friend, and that we often hurt those we love the most. As to the latter statement, it might be more accurate to say that we more often hurt those who love us the most. We don't hurt or lash out at those who love us though we think we will experience rejection from them. The next time you are curt with your parents (or your children or spouse, for that matter), think about whether you would have spoken that way to a client, or a member of your congregation, or someone with whom you were sharing your faith. Of course not. Why? Because you're trying to win them. You don't have to win family.

For me, I know beyond the shadow of a doubt that I could never reasonably say that in my childhood and teenage years it ever crossed my mind that my parents did not love me. They told me they did, over and over again—with a megaphone into my life. Whether it was showing up at sports games or concerts, Saturday night family nights, Sunday lunches, or my dad coming into my room—even after I had fallen asleep—every night to pray over me. We always knew we were loved. That's one of the reasons I pushed back so hard against them.

But that really isn't enough of an explanation. The truth was that, in my heart, I couldn't accept that my sin was forgiven. That I was, in fact, lovable—simply because I was a child of God. I understood the Christian world- and lifeview. I understood that we had been created in God's image, but I had not yet believed it.

And so, I spent most of my teenage years believing that the situation I found myself in was my parents' fault. It was my parents' fault that I was the one called on in Bible class at Charlotte Christian School to have the right answer. It was my parents' fault that, on more than one occasion when I was in trouble, adults looked at me and said, "Of all people, Ike, you should know better."

I remember one such occasion in high school. My buddies and I decided to skip church, go up to our friend's house, play basketball, and come back just before church ended. My dad could preach, and he could preach long. There was plenty of time to get in a few games of 2v2. So five of us piled into a little 280Z. Wouldn't you know it, as we are pulling out of the church parking lot along comes Brian's mom, ten minutes late for church. My friend's car was unmistakable. She flagged us down and we pulled over. I'm not sure how three teenage boys hid in the backseat of a tiny two-door sports car, but we gave it a shot. "Boys, what are you doing?" she asked as she came over. "I'm shocked," she said, "shocked and astonished," putting on all the grievance that a mom running ten minutes late for church could muster. "But you, Ike," she said, looking at me, "you should know better."

When we decided to drive my 1978 Toyota Tercel (lovingly named Mustard Vomit because of its color) into the hallways at school my senior year during exams, the headmaster pulled me into his office and said, "Ike, I understand why these other boys would do this, but I expected better from you." The backhanded compliment of expectation and responsibility. Why wouldn't you expect that from me? I'm just like them! Except when I'm not.

And so, when I had arrived at Covenant College as a freshman in 1993, it wasn't long before I found ways to "find out more about myself." To be sure, I had good friends who, in the midst of our explorations into drinking and the like, were believers who often tried to dig deeper into my growing disbelief with questions and with love. I'm forever grateful for Jackson and Dan, for Brandon and Teddy and Marshall, for challenging me in my growing teenage reality-bites-era nihilism. They covered for me, they lied for me (to keep me in school), and they tried to keep me from the edges I was approaching. When I drank, I drank hard. When I took a dare, I pushed the boundaries as hard as I could. By the time I was a sophomore in college, if anyone had thought to ask, I would seriously have told them I was not a Christian. "I understand it, I actually believe in it; I just don't want anything to do with it," I told the Campus Outreach coordinator the Christmas of my junior year.

I spent the Christmas conference in Orlando soaking in the hot tub, drinking Scotch from the hotel bar, and smoking cigarettes in defiance of the "rules."

When I left Covenant my junior year to study at Oxford University and lost that mitigating sanity of my Christian friends, I leaped into the pit with both feet. While I kept up my studies (the work ethic learned from my Scotch-Irish parents was strong), I pursued my own pleasures just as hard. The consequences of such a lifestyle eventually make themselves known. One morning, with no clear memory of the previous three days, I woke up in the gutter outside my apartment on Shoe Lane, sat up on the curb, and lit a cigarette. Newly minted as a twenty-one-year-old, I felt as though I were staring down at my own mortality.

The emotionalists always want to be an "old soul," while the "old souls" are always longing to feel "young again." I thought I had done and seen it all. If the feeling was less than accurate, the result was not. I talked to God that morning—prayed, really—but for the first time I actually started talking to God. "I don't know what this life is, God," I prayed, "but whatever it is I pretty much suck at it. I've always known I was a sinner and that I needed redemption, but what I really want right now is to be loved and to be able to give myself over to the perfect care of someone who loves me."

My dad says that there are people who come out after a sermon and say, "Preacher, that's the first time I've ever heard the gospel!" It can be a pretty big ego boost if your theology isn't in the right place. What that person is really saying is, "Preacher, the Holy Spirit opened the ears of my heart to hear the gospel today!"

That experience on this early April morning in the spring of 1996 was like that for me. I already knew four people who loved me unconditionally—my father, my mother, and my two sisters. But I couldn't accept that love until I had accepted that God actually loved me and that He had sent His Son—not just as a solution to a problem but because of that love. That morning, for the first time, I understood what love and lordship look like. I finally understood what C. S. Lewis meant when he said, "Fallen man is not simply an imperfect creature who needs improvement: he is a rebel who must lay down his arms." On that morning, I surrendered.

Rebel with a Cause

I'm a rebel. I rebel.
—Jyn Erso, *Rogue One*

Rebellion is a form of expression. It is an action that has an antecedent and an object. Something causes that rebellion, and it is almost always acted out against something or someone. What's the one "object" we all rebel against? God. After God is often authority. Parents are usually a close third and often serve as an amalgamation of the first two. The truth is that everything we rebel against after the first object is really just a proxy for the first one.

My rebellion took sin as its antecedent and almost always my parents as its object. Most of the time, I tried to convince myself that I rebelled because of an affront or a slight or from being crossed or misunderstood. I would then work it out by falling back on clichéd rationalizations: "I'm just being myself," or "If you can't accept me for who I am, then you must not love me."

The question then presents itself, How do people rebel? I think that, especially for youth and more especially for pastors' kids, there are two basic types of rebellion: covert rebellion and overt rebellion. My friend, if you're still reading this, I think you probably know exactly what I'm talking about. We start out with our covert rebellions, don't we? These rebellions play out quietly—online, in our heads, in fantasy worlds. We know we're supposed to say, "Yes, ma'am, and yes, sir; no, ma'am, and no, sir," but we want to start pushing our boundaries a little bit more.

To be sure, almost every kid in the history of mankind has practiced their covert rebellions. This is a common occurrence. Cain's sin didn't start with Adam in the field. Ask yourself, What was its antecedent? In many of these small, covert rebellions, we're just trying to build out a little space for ourselves, a little breathing room, a little room to grow. And most parents recognize this and understand it—most even harken back to when they were doing the same thing themselves.

But the covert rebellions of PKs can quickly become overt rebellions, even if we try to keep them hidden. Here is the key thing about rebellion for PKs: we're expected to be a perfect family. We're expected to have it all together. After all, a pastor is supposed to "[rule] his own house well" and "[have] his children in submission with all reverence" (1 Tim. 3:4). So what happens when my covert rebellion is noticed? It draws a response. When you forget to add the "sir" or "ma'am" to that response, someone in the church sees it, and guess what? They've got an opinion on your disrespect—and one they are likely to share.

Does this ever happen in your life? When there's that man in your church who has been looking for just the slightest chink in your father's armor (never mind that he's a hurting, broken sinner himself, probably trying to find significance for his own life), sees the slightest crack…and pounces. Or that woman who is trying to deal with her own pain who finally sees something outside of herself that she can point to and say, "It's not me! Finally! It's someone else's problem!" And she rationalizes, "It wouldn't be Christian of me not to bring it to my pastor's attention."

Your covert rebellion has just become overt rebellion. It has elicited a response. And now you're on a cycle that can be broken only by external intervention. You see, our rebellions are often more deeply seated in our own feelings of inadequacy and pain than we like to admit. We, as pastors' kids, want people to see us as we are and not as an appendage of our parents. We're not the only ones who go through this, certainly, but very few go through it in as public a setting as pastors' kids.

The two cycles have commenced. The cycle of covert rebellion has metastasized into overt rebellion. The cycle of response and recognition has commenced. Our rebellions have provoked a response, and, even if we know we're doing the wrong thing, even if we know it's bringing pain to our family or to those around us, we feel freedom, we feel agency. The freedom to be ourselves—set free from the limelight and gilded cage.

Hurting People Can Hurt People

The process of this cycle would be normal in most situations. In most situations, public interactions would be few and far between. You've probably got friends at school who act out, break the rules, challenge teachers constantly—you might even be one of them! But what I'm talking about is the rebellion that is unique to PKs. I'm talking about the type of rebellion that is built on expectations. That is a different type of rebellion altogether.

What do I mean? For all the rebellions of teenagers—on sports fields, in schools, and in neighborhoods—the rebellion that takes place in a church is unique. A sports field isn't designed for sinners, for broken and hurting people. There are always sinners on the athletic field—in fact, all of them are—but it isn't their hospital. The school is not designed for sinners—although it can teach sinners how to think Christianly. The neighborhood is full of sinners, but it isn't the neighborhood that was commissioned by God to be the body of Christ.

What or who is called to be the body of Christ? Well, that's the church. In other words, there's no one single place in all the world that specifically calls for people who—because of their faith—universally acknowledge that they do not have it all together. They don't just fail to have it all together, but everything they do in their own power is so completely saturated with sin that it is as dirty as the filthy "rags" we flush down a toilet.

The church is full of hurting people, and it is supposed to be a place where that hurt can be openly acknowledged and the love of God poured into old and new wounds of sin to provide healing. A place where the Balm of Gilead—the gospel of Jesus Christ—can be applied as a salve to open wounds caused by being a sinner and living in a sinful world.

That the church is a hospital for sinners, applying the life-giving electric shock of the resurrection of Jesus Christ, means that it is also a rehabilitation center, a place of hope. But in many cases the life-giving ministry of the gospel takes time to have an effect. And in the meantime, folks in the church are still working through their hurt and their pain. It means that what is supposed to be one of the few places in the world—if not the only place in the world—where true hope can be found can also become one of the places where the worst wounds are inflicted.

My young friend, you often experience this phenomenon to the greatest degree, second only to your parents. It takes time for people to heal, and the gospel—which promises us a new heart, a new home, and a new family—tells us clearly that Jesus has overcome the power of sin and invites us, by the Holy Spirit, to live out the process of overcoming the practice of sin. But who is the one telling all these people who have come to this particular church about this good news? Who is the one challenging them every Sunday to overcome, by the power of the Holy Spirit, their most deeply held sins—the ones that have ferreted and burrowed their way into our inmost core, our baby dragons that eat at our belief, the old man who tells us, "You're not good enough"? That's right, it's your dad. And when they can't lash out at him or his sweet wife, those hurting people can often find a new target.

You.

Remember the Face of Your Father

Where does this leave us? It is a hard thing to live in the gaze of expectation from all those eyes and observations. There simply is no way around it. You are in a unique situation, and, unless your father leaves the ministry for more private pastures, your childhood will be lived out and played out in front of anywhere from fifty to five thousand people. Sometimes you're going to want to run away from it. Sometimes you're going to glory in it. Sometimes you're going to hate the human mechanisms of it. You are going to be hurt. You are going to be a proxy target for your parents. People, in their own hurt and sinful natures, will probably never realize what they've put you through.

So, what do you do in the face of all that humanity? With living among saints and sinners? I am going to tell you the very thing that I hated to hear when I was your age: you must realize that you don't get your significance or your worth from them. You get it only from Christ. If you're struggling to figure out where you fit in, struggling to know why you matter outside of being "Pastor Smith's child," then you are actually in the same situation as all of humanity. We get our significance only from Christ. If you are not serving Him, you are serving only the "sovereign" self. And it is really easy to serve the sovereign self when it's in the guise of "finding myself." You can find yourself only by losing yourself in Christ. Jesus says, "For whoever desires to save his life will lose it, but whoever loses his life for My sake will find it" (Matt. 16:25).

Let me leave you with three simple pieces of advice.

Remember That Your Parents Are in the Fishbowl, Too

Yes, there is a difference between you and your parents. They chose to be in this situation, and you didn't. You are along for the ride. While that may lessen some of the impacts of the expectations of those watching your family, it doesn't disguise the fact that your father's job comes with a massive amount of pressure to always be "on his game," and your mother must navigate the treacherous waters of being a pastor's wife. They feel the same pressure you do.

Do you remember what I said at the beginning of this letter? Often the people we hurt are the people we know love us the most. In a weird, twisted way this seems the safest avenue to release our tensions and our pain. We can lash out and they won't run away. Sometimes your parents' quick comments, biting tone, and quick anger are not actually directed at you, but at themselves. To be sure, parents are called to discipline their children. What I'm talking about are the wounds we receive from wounded people. Mom and Dad take the sword thrusts, too. Just remember, when you're deciding whether to do that next thing, say that next word, lash out at them, or just flat-out disobey—they're under an unbelievable amount of pressure as well.

Remember That Your Faith Is Your Own

I doubt there are too many of you out there who are reading this book who feel as though you've got a free pass to heaven because of your parents. That isn't what I'm referring to by "Remember that your faith is your own." What I'm talking about is the need to have faith. As a pastor's kid, you probably do know the answers to a lot of those Bible class questions. In fact, you probably know more about theology and Scripture than some of the elders in your church.

The problem is that most of us start to depend on our intellectual knowledge of God. Learn, grow, study! These are good things! But don't forget that it is faith, repentance, and submission to Lordship that are ultimately required of us. You can be a good student of your father's teaching and not actually apprehend it.

Your faith must be your own, and you must own your faith. I remember my friend Michael Kruger telling me about a story he has often written and spoken of. When he was in his freshman year of college at UNC–Chapel Hill, he was in a religion class with Bart Ehrman, a famous critic of the authenticity of the Bible and the historical Jesus. The young Michael, confronted, challenged, and dismantled by this legendary intellect, had a decision to make. Would he fall under Dr. Ehrman's spell and begin to denounce all the things he had learned from his youth? Or would he accept this perspective as a challenge and grow in wisdom and knowledge, in favor with God and in favor with man? It was not Dr. Kruger's personal intellectual history that carried him through that moment. It was his faith in his personal Lord and Savior, Jesus Christ. Dr. Krueger is now the president of Reformed Theological Seminary in Charlotte, North Carolina, and one of the world's leading experts on the authenticity of the Bible. He regularly debates Dr. Ehrman and other revisionist critics with wit, intelligence, facts, and deeply personal faith.

So, ask yourself: Is this rebellion my expression of faith? In other words, am I actually trying to figure out whether this faith is mine? If the answer to that question is "Yes—I really don't know where I stand in relationship to God," then let me tell you something: there are more constructive (and significantly less damaging) ways to find that out than covertly or overtly rebelling against your parents, the instruction of God's Word, or the members of the congregation. Be honest, but be respectful. Remember that you live in your father's house and that you are currently only a visitor in your Father's house. Be willing to pray and ask God to show Himself to you. I promise you—He will. God always shows up.

Remember That "Now" Choices Have "Then" Consequences

I praise the Lord that despite my rebellious youth, I was spared from going too far down the path of destruction. I drank too much, smoked too much, dabbled in drugs occasionally (though I really didn't care for them), and used language that I knew would cause sailors to blush. God kept me from doing any lasting physical harm to myself, even though I had friends who did. But I did do psychological harm. I learned that I took everything to extremes. I set patterns for myself in my teens and early twenties that still, to this day, frighten me.

I know that apart from Christ, that's the person I am. I go out of my way not to abuse others, but I find every way to abuse myself. In my late twenties, I went through a destructive relationship. God had one more major idol to get out of my life—the idol of love. It took over five years for God to break me down completely, and it was not pretty. In the middle of it all, when my faith had dwindled and I had pushed the Holy Spirit as far away from me as I dared, I dove back into the lifestyle of my late teens. This time I didn't just pursue the alcohol and the nicotine; I also pursued ungodly companionship. I made significant mistakes.

Thankfully, God pulled me out of that mire and set me back on the pathway of His Word due to the love of my family in large part and to a life-threatening illness. Several years later, when I was thirty-five, I experienced God's kindest providence to me outside of my salvation and family in meeting my wife, Angie, and her two children, Win and Virginia. I am an incredibly blessed man. But remember this: there came a point when I had to look into the eyes of this remarkable woman and tell her about my past. It was not a comfortable moment, and certainly not one I want for you. And yet it became a moment when Christ yet again demonstrated His love with Angie's compassion.

Let me be clear: rebellion does not provide anything positive that can be taken into new, healthy relationships. Do not buy into the world's idea that those experiences "shape us" or give us "real-world experience." There is nothing I learned from my sin that God's Word had not already told me. Rebellion and sin have real-life, long-term consequences, and none of them are good. I live with those every day.

Thank God we have a Savior who can redeem those consequences.

Remember the Benefits of Being in a Pastor's Family

Finally, forget none of His benefits. It is hard in the midst of pain and the expectations of the congregation to remember this fact: God has called you and your family to a high calling, and it is in many ways a difficult, painful journey. But it is also one that provides its own unique brand of benefits. The shepherd often has many sheep to curl up around him to keep him warm on cold nights. You have the benefit of seeing people brought into the family of God.

While we know the church is full of hurting people, I would also remind you that the church is full of sinners saved by grace and that God has charged your family to care for them. Even more inconceivable is that He charges them to care for you. When you can maintain the healthy balance that such a relationship necessitates, there are a thousand different ways the flock cares for the shepherd, too. I could truly write another whole chapter on the benefits of being a pastor's kid in a pastor's family.

Don't Inherit the Wind

In the book of Proverbs, God tells us, "He who troubles his own house will inherit the wind, and the fool will be servant to the wise of heart" (Prov. 11:29). I haven't used a lot of Scripture verses in this letter. If you are, as I imagine you to be, a young pastor's son or daughter in your teenage years, you've probably heard and read all the verses about honoring your parents, listening to your father, and not neglecting the wisdom of your mother's years. To be sure, God clearly gives us a command to honor our father and mother in the Ten Commandments, the moral law that undergirds His creation and was fulfilled—but not abolished—by Jesus Christ.

Consider it from a slightly different perspective, though. The family is a mandate of creation—a creation ordinance that was given to us by God as the mechanism to bring good into the world and into your life. Is it under the curse of the fall? Certainly. Does God give us protections as children when that family unit becomes harmful? Absolutely. But you always need to be asking yourself the question: Am I the one bringing ruin my family? Do not be the person who inherits only the wind.

No, we have a better inheritance—as sons and daughters of a greater family: the family of God. And in the pastor's family, the human and the divine families are brought together in a special and unique way.

> O LORD, You are the portion of my inheritance and my cup;
> You maintain my lot.
> The lines have fallen to me in pleasant places;
> Yes, I have a good inheritance. (Ps. 16:5–6)

Your brother in Christ,
Ike

Ike Reeder is the president of Birmingham Theological Seminary, son of Pastor Harry Reeder of Briarwood Presbyterian Church, husband to Angie, and stepdad of Virginia and Win.

FINANCIAL CRISIS
High Calling with a High Price

Daniel Wakefield

God gave us Daniel when John was just two years into the ministry. He was our third child and would soon learn that hand-me-downs and sharing were our way of life. It was a small church with few resources. But there was plenty of love from God's people, and Dan thrived in that environment. The following years would produce a young boy wrapped up with typical boyhood fascination with dinosaurs. This would develop into an absorbing interest in reptiles that would lead to undergraduate degrees in biology and education. In the midst of his education, God reached down and saved Dan, and he became willing to give it all up in order to serve Christ.

In the providence of God, he has been called to be a pastor in Christ's church. His training is now focused on ministering to God's people. He and his wife, Bethany, have two young boys, William and Benjamin, and a daughter, Susanna. We are thankful for all that God has done in his life and look prayerfully to see what the Lord may accomplish through him.

Warmly,
John and Cathy Wakefield

Dear Pastor's Kid,

I think it's fair to say that all of us PKs have been there at one time or another. Christmastime rolls around, and that present you'd really been hoping for isn't under the tree. You couldn't go to that playoff game, or your vacation wasn't quite as exciting as the one your friend went on. Do you know what I'm talking about? There are usually things the average pastor can't afford. Maybe there have been times when things actually got tough. If your dad is involved in planting a church, you know exactly what I'm talking about. Unless he has been sent out from a large, wealthy congregation that can fully support him, you're probably conscious of the tight financial situation you will be in, at least until the time when the church is up and running. It might even be a long-term situation if your dad pastors a small church. But maybe you've experienced something much more serious than that. There are times when pastors are unjustly removed from their position at a church. If you have experienced this, you know that finances can be a significant source of concern and challenge for your parents (and even you) during such a time.

Whatever your situation might be, I want to begin my letter by saying this: I've been there, maybe not in every exact situation that you have been, but I remember what it's like to be in small churches. I know what it feels like to have my dad removed from church office and left wondering how he's going to support our family. I have also been involved in a church plant and seen my dad work jobs on the side to help make ends meet. There are times when life just isn't easy, and when tough situations happen in the church, the pastor is often the one caught in the crosshairs.

Please know that I am not writing to tell you that it's fine to be depressed about all this. While I can fully empathize with your situation, I do think it would be wrong for us to dwell on the things we don't have, simply because our dad's salary wasn't as big as that of some of our peers' dads. Without trying to minimize the difficulty of going through some tough situations, I think it would be a terrible tragedy for either of us to come away from this letter feeling only regret or having a bitter attitude toward those who may have contributed to the financial burdens. In fact, I think we should come away from this letter feeling the very opposite. The truth is, I believe we have some great reasons to be thankful.

Things to Consider

Picture yourself walking into a courtroom during an important trial. It's a public trial, so you can slip into the back of the room and watch purely as an onlooker. The defendant is there, ready to be put on trial. The attorneys are looking over their notes for the case. The jury is ready to hear testimonies. The whole room smells like dusty law books and justice. Suddenly, the judge enters, all in the courtroom rise, and proceedings begin. Coming in with the assumption of a fair trial, what would you think if the judge and the jury were to hear only one side of the case? Only the prosecuting attorney could present their side of the story. It would be impossible to come to a just decision on the case, wouldn't it?

There can certainly be tough financial times when your dad is a pastor. No question about it. But what if that were the only side of the story we were to consider? Like the judge and jury, we wouldn't have a balanced viewpoint. Our perception would be skewed, and we might be tempted to have a negative attitude about life as a PK. So, I want you to consider a few things with me, things that will help us see the situation in a more profitable light. Let's allow the defense attorney to say a few words so that we can make a better judgment.

Thinking of Others First

It's fair to assume that the pastor is unlikely to have the largest salary in the church, so it's probable that you have friends whose parents can afford to give them things that you can't have or take them to places you can't afford to go. Continually dwelling on these things blinds us to a valid point. Although the pastor's family isn't likely to be the richest one in the congregation, it's typically not the poorest one, either. The next time you go to church, I would encourage you to lift up your eyes and look around you. There's a good chance some families in attendance are having a much harder financial time than yours. If we allow ourselves to feel only pity for ourselves, we will miss out on a wonderful opportunity to practice and experience something very important: compassion.

Have you been both the giver and the recipient of compassion? I'm sure your parents, among others, have displayed it to you. It's a remarkable feeling when someone reaches out to help during a time of need. It evidences a heart that sympathizes or empathizes with your situation, doesn't it?

Maybe your parents stayed all night with you in the hospital after surgery or spent hours helping you with homework you didn't really understand. Why did they do this? Because they care about you. They looked beyond themselves and their own needs and considered yours, despite any inconveniences it brought their way. That principle is remarkably important; the apostle Paul told the Philippian church, "Let nothing be done through selfish ambition or conceit, but in lowliness of mind let each esteem others better than himself. Let each of you look out not only for his own interests, but also for the interests of others" (Phil. 2:3–4). Yes, you might be facing some difficult financial circumstances, but typically there are others who have it worse. Consider how you might show compassion to those who have less than yourself and display the spirit of one who has been shown compassion by Christ. Keep your mind focused outwardly; when you are inclined to think *Woe is me!*, lift up your eyes and look to those who are less privileged than you. You will find it a balm to your soul to take the focus off yourself and find true joy in focusing on others.

Putting Your Hope in the Wrong Thing

Have you ever cheered for a sports team in a playoff game, only to be disappointed because they "let you down" and lost the game? Or have you been particularly excited about seeing a movie, only to find out that it wasn't nearly as good as you had thought it would be? In both cases, you could say that you had put your hope in the wrong thing. Your hope was not rewarded. I want to make sure you consider the same thing about finances. Yes, it's good to be a wise steward of money. And yes, it's difficult when you don't have enough of it, but, just like anyone else, a PK can fall into the trap of putting their money in the wrong basket (literally). We can think to ourselves, "If only my dad made a little more money, I'd be able to get (insert latest gadget)." We can think, "If only I had some more money, I could do all the things my friends get to do." This may seem like a bit of harmless daydreaming, but be careful; that's exactly what Satan wants you to believe.

Remember the parable Jesus told about the man who stored up all his wealth into barns (Luke 12:13–21)? He thought he had enough for years to come. He thought he was set for life. He could now retire and travel to all the places he'd been wanting to go. He could "take [his] ease, eat, drink, and be merry." But he forgot one important detail: he wasn't ready to die. He thought he was ready to live the rest of his life, but he didn't realize how soon his life would be cut short. And just like having a sports team let you down, all of his wealth let him down. No matter how much he gained, it didn't prepare him for eternity.

Jesus told people in the context of that parable, "Take heed and beware of covetousness, for one's life does not consist of the abundance of the things he possesses." Have you ever thought that if you could have a bit more stuff, your life would be much happier? If that is the constant pattern of your thoughts, you are putting your hope in something that has no eternal foundation. Paul told his son in the faith, Timothy, "Those who desire to be rich fall into temptation and a snare, and into many foolish and harmful lusts which drown men in destruction and perdition" (1 Tim. 6:9). I'm writing this to you as an older brother; don't fall into the trap of putting your hope in the wrong thing.

Love Is Better

Being overly discouraged about financial issues can also cause us to miss out on another important matter. Your family might be having a difficult time financially. But is there love in your home? Do your parents love each other? Do they love you and your siblings? Do you love your siblings (even if they occasionally get on your nerves)? If that is the case, then you possess wealth that no amount of money could ever buy.

In the book of Proverbs, Solomon was teaching his sons important principles for living wisely in this life. And although he taught them about the wise use of money, he also taught them not to put their hope in it. But he went beyond just warning his sons. He also wanted to convince them that there is something better. He said to them, "Better is a dinner of herbs where love is, than a fatted calf with hatred" (Prov. 15:17). Take a moment to think about those two situations. In one home, there may be a family that is incredibly affluent. The dad is a CEO for some major company and has a six-figure income. Their house is practically a mansion. They drive BMWs and Land Rovers. They vacation regularly in exotic places. Their kids have all the latest gadgets and are some of the most popular kids at school.

Sounds pretty appealing, doesn't it? But here's the problem: nine times out of ten, there is little love in that type of home. The parents are often fighting about something. Typically (though not always), the kids don't respect their parents. It's a rare thing to walk into such a setting where a sense of entitlement doesn't penetrate every area of their lives. In reality, all that stuff doesn't seem so important, does it?

Think with me about the other family. Dad has a job, though it doesn't provide the six-figure salary. He makes enough to put food on the table and pay the bills, but that's about it. Any vacations they take are short and usually somewhere fairly local. They drive an older car that seems to have a long history of trouble. They can't afford to give their kids all the latest gadgets, and their dinners are often simple meals made from whatever was on sale at the grocery store. But here's the crux of the matter: if there is *love* in that family, the abundance consists not in what they have externally but in the relationships that bind them together. If you were to sit with them at their dinner table, you'd hear laughter and good conversations more often than not. The parents evidently love one another. They love their kids and seek to be involved in their lives, and the kids love their parents and each other. Of course, it's not a sinless environment, but the basic principle of love is the dominating characteristic of the home. Which situation is more preferable? Solomon didn't hesitate. Choose the home where love is found.

Some of my fondest memories growing up were of Sunday evenings after church with my family. We would eat together and then hang out in the living room. My dad would be exhausted from a long day of preaching and ministering to people, and we would sit around and talk about anything and everything. School, relationships, vacations—you name it, we probably talked about it. Sometimes, in his exhausted state, my dad would start laughing about something that wasn't even really that funny, and soon the ripple effect of a contagious laugh would ensue. That's not exactly the world's definition of happiness, but I wouldn't trade those times for all the riches in the world. Yes, there were many times when we sinned against one another and had to reconcile. There's no such thing as a perfect family, even if you're a pastor's family. We certainly didn't have everything, but we had each other—and that was plenty.

Financial Struggles Are an Opportunity

There is one final point I would ask you to consider before pondering a little practical application. Learning to trust God is a righteous thing. He is overwhelmingly trustworthy, and placing our trust in Him will never result in disappointment. At the risk of sounding as though we relish poverty, financial difficulties are a wonderful, God-given opportunity to learn to grow in our trust of Him. I wonder if you have ever thought about that before. Jesus told His disciples that they shouldn't worry about what they were going to eat or what clothes they were going to put on. Instead, they were to trust that God would provide for their needs. He said to them, "Seek first the kingdom of God and His righteousness, and all these things shall be added to you" (Matt. 6:33). The question is, Do you believe Him? It's really quite easy to believe some of these things when there's an abundance of money. It's a lot harder when resources are tight. But isn't our God the same God regardless of the circumstances we find ourselves in? Financial difficulties are one of the schools used by God to teach us to trust Him. Let's not waste that opportunity.

Now What?

It certainly is helpful to hear both sides of a story. But where should you go from here? What does this all look like when practically applied? I'm sure your dad is good at coming up with three points for a lot of situations. And since you're probably used to that, let's consider three things to focus on. You might call them exhortations or applications. You might even call this a "to-do list." These aren't things I've dreamed up; rather, they are clear guidelines delineated in Scripture.

Learn to Be Content

I have a love/hate relationship with math. I was good at it in high school, but the subject matter quickly got beyond my capabilities in college, and

I just wanted to be done with it for good. Have you ever been stuck on a math word problem? They seem to be the thing that everyone hates the most in math. It's particularly bad if you misunderstand that word problem. You are almost certainly doomed to get a big fat *0* if you didn't comprehend the concept behind the problem.

The same thing can happen with the Bible. If you misunderstand a verse or passage, it will be almost impossible to come away with the right application. I believe this to be a regular occurrence with Philippians 4:13. I'm sure you're familiar with the verse: "I can do all things through Christ who strengthens me." This verse is often quoted as a motivational verse for accomplishing great things in life as a Christian: "I can win the high school football championship through Christ who strengthens me," or "I can get an *A* on this test through Christ who strengthens me," or "I can get a promotion at my job through Christ who strengthens me."

Let's take a closer look at the context of this verse (vv. 11–13): "Not that I speak in regard to need, for I have learned in whatever state I am, to be content: I know how to be abased, and I know how to abound. Everywhere and in all things I have learned both to be full and to be hungry, both to abound and to suffer need. I can do all things through Christ who strengthens me."

Paul wasn't talking in verse 13 about doing anything conceivable. In this passage, he was talking about the various states of *financial and material need* he had experienced. Sometimes he had experienced abundance and hadn't been in need of anything. Other times he was facing situations where he was going hungry because the money just wasn't there. Surely that was challenging. No one likes to go hungry. We all have a desire to see our needs met. But what was Paul's attitude? He had learned to be content no matter what circumstance he was currently experiencing. He wasn't spending his days worrying about what clothes he was going to wear, or what food he was going to eat, or the quality of vacation he was going on. If there was plenty of food on the table, and lots of money in the bank, he was thankful and content. If there was only a crust of bread to eat, and the money was almost gone, he was still thankful and content. His life wasn't marked by complaining and worry. It was marked by contentment.

How did he do that? We all know how difficult it is to be content when finances are tight and we can't buy or do the things we want. So, what was Paul's secret? How could he be content no matter what his circumstances were? He tells us in verse 13. "No matter what situation I am in," Paul says, "I can be content through Christ, who strengthens me." So, it's not that I can win the football game; it's that I can be content whether I win or lose the football game, through Christ who strengthens me. It's not that I can get the promotion; it's that I can be content whether I get it or not, through Christ who strengthens me. And more along the lines of this letter, it's not that I can get out of this difficult financial situation; it's that I can be content in whatever financial situation I find myself, through Christ who strengthens me. Contentment is hard. But Christ's strength is an ever-flowing fountain to those who depend on Him. And, as Paul says to Timothy in another letter, "Godliness with contentment is *great gain*" (1 Tim. 6:6, emphasis added).

Lay Up Treasure in Heaven

I'm sure you've saved up to buy something before. We all have. Maybe it was a bike that you really wanted, or perhaps a new video game, tickets to a concert, or a musical instrument. The point is that we save up to buy things we value. We wouldn't buy them if we didn't think they would hold significant value to us. And while saving up for things like that is a natural endeavor, Jesus tells His followers there is a vastly more worthy kind of saving we should be doing, and it has nothing to do with earthly things. Listen to what Jesus says in Matthew 6:19–21: "Do not lay up for yourselves treasures on earth, where moth and rust destroy and where thieves break in and steal; but lay up for yourselves treasures in heaven, where neither moth nor rust destroys and where thieves do not break in and steal. For where your treasure is, there your heart will be also."

It doesn't seem as though Jesus is prohibiting the wise stewardship of our resources or saving up a down payment to buy a house, or even saving up to get the musical instrument we've been wanting. It would seem that what Jesus has in mind is an overall heart attitude about money and possessions that leads to a life filled with making certain kinds of decisions. To summarize it in one word, Jesus is warning His disciples against *worldliness*. As I previously noted, it can be easy to fall into the trap of putting our hope in money and possessions. That's what Jesus is talking about here. Listen to what J. C. Ryle says about these verses in *Expository Thoughts on Matthew*: "Where are our hearts? What do we love best? Are our [greatest] affections on things in earth, or things in heaven? Life or death depends on the answer we can give to these questions. If our treasure is earthly, our hearts will be earthly also."

What is your attitude toward money and earthly possessions? Do you feel as though you will die if you can't get that thing you have been saving up for? Do you feel as though your life will end if you don't get some more money so you can do the things your friends are doing? If the answer is yes, those are pretty good indicators that your treasure is in the wrong place.

On the other hand, Jesus tells His disciples to store up treasure in heaven. As you think about the financial struggles that may characterize a pastor's family, you need to remember that there is something that cannot be quantified coming for those who trust in Jesus. The wealth of this world seems attractive, but remember what Jesus said: the treasures of this world can be destroyed or stolen. Money can be taken or spent. Possessions grow old, break, and may be stolen, but the treasures of heaven can never be taken away. Matthew Henry wrote in his commentary on this passage, "There are treasures in heaven, as sure as there are on this earth; and those in heaven are the only true treasures, the riches and glories and pleasures that are at God's right hand, which those that are sanctified truly arrive at, when they come to be sanctified perfectly."

Doesn't that sound infinitely better than the treasures this world has to offer? After all, what earthly "thing" ever really satisfied you, anyway? You spend months hoping for that new thing, then you get it and it's great—and then the novelty wears off and you start wanting the next latest item. The things of this world simply don't satisfy. Christ and Christ alone can fill that void. Live in such a way that your life demonstrates the reality of Christ's fullness to the world.

Be Generous

In 2 Corinthians 8, the apostle Paul described a crisis situation. There was a serious famine in the land of Judea. People were starving. The believers there were suffering, and Paul was encouraging the believers in Corinth to contribute financially to the work. He wanted them to express their love and unity with these believers by helping in the relief effort. This may have been difficult for some of them. Maybe they didn't have additional resources lying around to give away. Paul didn't command them to give (like a tax) but urged them to give voluntarily from the heart as an act of love. Notice Paul's words to the Corinthians. He referenced the example of the Christians in the region of Macedonia. Listen to what he wrote: "Moreover, brethren, we make known to you the grace of God bestowed on the churches of Macedonia; that in a great trial of affliction the abundance of their joy and their deep poverty abounded in the riches of their liberality. For I bear witness that according to their ability, yes, and beyond their ability, they were freely willing, imploring us with much urgency that we would receive the gift and the fellowship of the ministering to the saints" (vv. 1–4).

These Macedonian Christians overflowed in their generosity to give to people who were suffering. No big deal, right? I'm sure we've all known some generous people. But look what Paul said about them. There were *extremely poor*. That changes your perspective, doesn't it? These people barely had two nickels to rub together in their pockets, and yet they were giving for the sake of others. But that's not all. It's not just that they were giving; they were *begging* Paul for the chance to give. They were ready to give their money and themselves to do whatever they could to help their brothers and sisters in Christ. When you consider the financial situation they were in themselves, that's a pretty incredible character trait. They were a living example of Paul's statement, "God loves a cheerful giver."

So, what does this have to do with you? How does it relate to your family's struggles with finances? Simple: be generous. Generosity isn't dependent on the state of your bank account. You don't have to wait until you're rich to be a cheerful giver. Generosity begins with a state of mind that says, "All that I have belongs to God."

What kind of motivation can give you the ability to be generous even when things aren't going as well as you'd like them to? How can you be a cheerful giver when the bank account isn't overflowing? Paul told the Corinthian believers, "For you know the grace of our Lord Jesus

Christ, that though He was rich, yet for your sake He became poor, so that you through His poverty might become rich" (v. 9).

We can be generous as believers because God in Christ has been overwhelmingly generous to us. In *The Happy Christian*, David Murray writes, "When we give sacrificially, painfully, and lovingly, we draw a small-scale picture of the gospel message."

God the Son left His rightful position in the glory of heaven to condescend to us. He left His riches to become poor, and He did it for you and me. If that is true, how can we not be generous to others? The gospel should motivate us to give because God Himself has given so freely to us. That's something we can rejoice over, no matter what circumstances we find ourselves in.

These three things I've shared aren't complicated, but they certainly are challenging. The fact is, we can't do them apart from the supernatural help of God. This is why Paul said, "I can do all things through Christ who strengthens me." Don't buy into the lie that you are able to do this alone. Having an attitude of trust in the midst of financial difficulties isn't about the power of positive thinking. It's about depending on the Lord for His grace. And thankfully, there is an abundance of grace for those who trust Him.

Your brother in Christ,
Daniel

Daniel was born in 1985 into a pastor's family in Ontario, Canada. His father pastored a few churches while he was growing up in Ontario, Ohio, and Mississippi. Daniel pursued a degree in biology and has worked as a high school teacher as well as in the field of photography. Daniel is married to his wife, Bethany, and has three children. In his spare time, he enjoys spending time with his family and doing wildlife photography. His photos can be viewed at www.wakefieldwildlife.com.

AFTERWORD

As I sit here to add a few words in conclusion, we find ourselves as a nation in the midst of a global pandemic. When I began this book, such a scenario would have seemed a million miles away. Has that changed the scenarios that PKs now find themselves in? Perhaps to a degree, or at least in some temporary measure, but the reality is there is nothing new under the sun, and the words of this book have a timeless sense of wisdom that will flow down through the ages.

We have six children. They range in age from twenty-three all the way down to six. It has felt like I am the eternal diaper changer who has never stopped teaching her children to read. On the other hand, that wide range of ages has also allowed Neil and me to watch the lives of our PKs unfold in a variety of ways. They have all responded to life in the goldfish bowl in a different manner. We have an introvert, an extreme extrovert, and everything in between. And we still haven't attained the goal of producing the perfect PK! That's what keeps us on our knees. In that sense, you are no different from any other child of God. And that is the big takeaway from this book: there will never be a "one-size-fits-all" book for kids living under the roof of the ministry home, nor is there a front-cover perfection of what you are supposed to look like. So why address the PK at all? Well, the reality is that there are dozens of books written for pastors and preachers and missionaries, all of which address the unique challenges and opportunities they face in their calling.

Not so for you, their offspring! You all face ministry situations that you generally can't discuss with your peers for fear that you will let your parents down, sound as though you are less holy than you think you should be, or simply don't want to be the "voice of your father." I well remember our oldest daughter working in a coffee shop in Savannah, Georgia. She would often tend to customers in the drive-through. On countless occasions she would come home, having met people who would identify her as "Neil Stewart's daughter." Initially this was something she was proud of. She had been an only child for nearly seven years and had developed a close bond with her daddy. Before long, however, she simply wanted to fade into oblivion and be known as Hannah. Not an unreasonable expectation, but one that was not likely to happen, especially as she is a walking female version of her daddy! The words of this book would have served her well had she been able to purchase a copy back then.

There is no escaping the fact that you, too, are in a unique situation. The question is, Will you choose to focus on the immediate and many challenges and blessings, or the fact that you are on a journey that others will never have the opportunity to tread? That journey is not a catwalk where you are expected to display your best persona now. It is a pathway through mountaintops and deep, deep, valleys; one that will afford you joys that few others will ever experience and one that will impel you to delve deeper into pain that many will not suffer. We are all born with a natural propensity to fall into one of two categories: we either see every silver lining having a cloud or every cloud having a silver lining. I realize that this book will be read by both alike, though it will probably be more challenging to the former group. It is for you especially that I long to see a deeper trust in Christ as a result of listening to the voices in these pages.

The Lord is a good God, a gracious King, and a loving heavenly Father who has ordained every day of your life. From the beginning of all eternity, He had mapped out the minutia of who your parents would be, the fact that your earthly father would be called to devote his life to the service of Christ in full-time Christian ministry, and that you would spend the entirety of your childhood under that umbrella. Not only did He do that for the flock your father now ministers to, He did it for *you*! If God has made a mistake and placed you in a life situation when you ought really to have found ultimate happiness in a different family, outside the realm of ministry life, then the words of

Romans 8:28 have fallen to the ground, void. And yet we *know* that is not the case. You are in the very best place you could possibly be. Your Father has never once wandered from His purposes for your life: to give you a future and a hope. My prayer for you is that you will find these words to be true and that in doing so you will be able to lift your voice to heaven and find not only contentment but immeasurable joy as you press on into the kingdom, laying hold of Christ and using this gift of ministry life for the betterment of your soul and that of others.

Press on!
Catherine